A YEARLONG BIBLE STUDY GUIDE:

52 WEEK BIBLE SUMMARY OF SCRIPTURE FOR BEGINNERS

WRITTEN BY

REV MINTON THOMAS

Copyright © 2024 Rev Minton Thomas Publishing ™

A Yearlong Bible Study Guide for Beginners: 52 Week Bible Summary of Scripture

All rights reserved. No part of this publication may be reproduced, distributed, or transmitted in any form or by any means, including photocopying, recording, or other electronic or mechanical methods, without the prior written permission of the publisher, except in the case of brief quotations embodied in critical reviews and certain other noncommercial uses permitted by copyright law.

Scripted and Published by Rev Minton Thomas.

For more information, or to contact us go to **https://beacons.ai/revthomas**

Book & Cover design by Rev Minton Thomas

First Edition: August 2024

PREFACE

A Journey of Discovery

As you embark on this yearlong journey through the Bible, remember that it is not just an academic exercise but a spiritual exploration. Each book of the Bible contributes to a larger story of God's love, redemption, and promise. Allow the Scriptures to challenge, inspire, and transform you as you discover the richness of God's Word.

This guide is a companion on your journey, aiming to make the Bible more approachable and meaningful. Whether you are seeking answers, desiring spiritual growth, or simply exploring the richness of Scripture, may this yearlong study be a source of enlightenment and encouragement.

May this study be a source of spiritual enrichment and growth as you explore the timeless wisdom and profound truths of the Bible.

Welcome to your yearlong adventure in Scripture. May it be transformative and illuminating as you discover the depth of God's love and the breadth of His promises.

Blessings on your journey,

TABLE OF CONTENTS

Introduction

Welcome to A Yearlong Bible Study Guide: 52 Week Bible Summary of Scripture for Beginners. This guide is designed to walk you through the profound journey of understanding the Bible, offering a structured approach to exploring its vast and rich content.

Whether you are new to the Bible or seeking a fresh perspective, this guide aims to make your study experience both accessible and transformative.

The Bible, composed of the Old and New Testaments, is the cornerstone of Christian faith and tradition. It tells the story of God's relationship with humanity, unfolding through diverse literary genres, historical accounts, poetry, prophecy, and profound teachings.

For beginners, navigating this expansive text can be overwhelming. This guide simplifies the journey by providing weekly summaries that capture the essence of each biblical book, helping you grasp the overarching narrative and key messages.

PURPOSE OF THE GUIDE

This guide is crafted to:

- Offer Clarity: Provide clear and concise summaries of each book of the Bible, making it easier to understand the major themes, characters, and events.

- Encourage Reflection: Include thought-provoking questions and prompts to help you engage deeply with the text and apply its lessons to your life.

- Enhance Understanding: Offer explanations of challenging terms and concepts, aiding in a richer comprehension of the biblical context.

- Foster Growth: Equip you with a structured plan to read through the Bible in a year, fostering spiritual growth and a deeper connection with Scripture.

HOW TO USE THIS GUIDE

The guide is organized into weekly sections, each focusing on a specific book of the Bible. For each week, you will find:

- A Summary: A brief overview of the book of the bible

- Key Characters and Events: Highlighted figures and significant occurrences that shape the narrative.

- Key Teachings: Important lessons and theological insights as well as contextual and historical information to enrich your understanding.

TO FULLY BENEFIT FROM THIS GUIDE:

- Set Aside Regular Time: Dedicate a specific time each week for your study. Consistency will help you build a habit and deepen your understanding.

- Reflect and Journal: Use the reflection questions to journal your thoughts and insights. This practice can enhance personal growth and spiritual development.

- Pray for Guidance: Begin your study with prayer, asking for insight and understanding as you read and reflect on the Scriptures.

Genesis

BOOK SUMMARY:

Genesis, the foundational book of the Bible, is an epic narrative that unveils the origins of the universe, humanity, and God's redemptive plan. Authored by Moses under divine inspiration, it chronicles the creation of the heavens, the earth, and all living beings, culminating in the formation of the first human beings, Adam and Eve. The book establishes the narrative of God's covenant relationship with His creation and lays the groundwork for understanding the intricate tapestry of Scripture that follows.

Within the pages of Genesis, we witness the breathtaking act of God's creative power as He speaks the universe into existence, fashioning a perfect, harmonious world. The narrative then focuses on the Garden of Eden, a paradise where Adam and Eve enjoyed intimate fellowship with their Creator, living in perfect communion with Him and all of creation. However, their disobedience and subsequent fall into sin ushered in a world marred by pain, suffering, and spiritual separation from God.

The consequences of sin are vividly portrayed through the stories of Cain and Abel, the genealogies leading up to Noah, and the account of the great flood, which serves as a powerful reminder of God's judgment on sin and His grace in preserving a remnant. The narrative continues with the dispersion of nations at the Tower of Babel, setting the stage for God's covenant with Abraham and the formation of the nation of Israel.

The latter half of Genesis chronicles the lives of the patriarchs – Abraham, Isaac, Jacob, and Joseph – highlighting God's faithfulness to His promises and His sovereign orchestration of events. Through these narratives, we witness the struggles, triumphs, and faith journeys of these pivotal figures, as God's redemptive plan begins to unfold.

Woven throughout the book are profound themes of creation, the nature of humanity made in God's image, the devastating impact of sin, the promise of redemption through the offspring of the woman (foreshadowing the coming of the Messiah, Jesus Christ), and the establishment of God's covenant relationship with His chosen people.

Genesis lays the foundation for the entire biblical narrative, providing the essential context for understanding God's character, His purposes, and His eternal plan of salvation, which reaches its climax in the New Testament with the coming of Christ.

KEY EVENTS, CHARACTERS, AND TEACHINGS:

- The six days of creation and the establishment of the Sabbath, highlighting God's creative power and the significance of rest (Genesis 1-2:3)

- The formation of Adam and Eve, made in God's image as the crown of creation, and their role as stewards over the earth (Genesis 2:4-25)

- The temptation, disobedience, and fall in the Garden of Eden, introducing sin and its consequences into the world (Genesis 3:1-24)

- The story of Cain and Abel, highlighting the effects of sin, jealousy, and the importance of obedience and right worship (Genesis 4)

- The genealogies tracing the line of Seth and the increasing wickedness of humanity (Genesis 5)

- The account of Noah and the great flood, showcasing God's judgment on sin and His grace in preserving a remnant (Genesis 6-9)

- The Tower of Babel and the dispersion of nations, revealing humanity's pride and God's sovereignty over languages and borders (Genesis 11)

- The call of Abram (later Abraham) and God's covenant promise to make him a great nation and a blessing to all peoples (Genesis 12)

- The lives of the patriarchs: Abraham's journey of faith, the birth of Isaac, the near-sacrifice of Isaac, and God's provision (Genesis 12-25)

- The account of Isaac, his struggle with infertility, and the birth of Jacob and Esau (Genesis 25-28)

- Jacob's journey, his wrestle with God, his name change to Israel, and the birth of his twelve sons (Genesis 28-35)

- The story of Joseph, his betrayal by his brothers, his rise to power in Egypt, and his forgiveness and reconciliation (Genesis 37-50)

EXPLORING SOME DEEPER MEANINGS:

1. The literary structure and parallelisms in the creation account point to God's intentional design. For instance, the repeated phrase "and there was evening, and there was morning" highlights the cyclical nature of creation and the establishment of the seven-day week. The parallelism between the first three days (forming the realms) and the next three days (filling those realms) reveals an intricate pattern and order.

2. The Garden of Eden is described using rich imagery and metaphors that convey spiritual truths about humanity's relationship with God before sin entered the world. The garden itself represents a sacred space where God dwelt with His creation. The "tree of life" symbolizes the eternal life and sustenance that comes from obedience to God.

3. The serpent's temptation of Eve demonstrates the subtle tactics of deception that appeal to human desires for wisdom, autonomy, and self-exaltation. The serpent's questioning of God's command plants seeds of doubt, while the promise of being "like God" exploits humanity's desire for power and knowledge apart from the Creator.

4. The trees in the Garden, the "tree of life" and the "tree of the knowledge of good and evil," represent the choice between obedience (leading to life) and disobedience (leading to death). This symbolism underscores the consequences of human rebellion against God's design and authority.

5. The protevangelium in Genesis 3:15, "he will crush your head, and you will strike his heel," is the first messianic prophecy in Scripture. It foreshadows the eventual victory of the Messiah (Christ) over Satan and the redemption of humanity from the consequences of sin. This verse plants the seed for God's redemptive plan that will unfold throughout the rest of the Bible.

6. The story of Cain and Abel explores the profound effects of sin on human relationships, including jealousy, murder, and the breakdown of familial bonds. It also introduces the concept of being one's "brother's keeper," emphasizing the responsibility to care for and protect others, which is a reflection of God's character.

7. The genealogies in Genesis 5 and 11 reveal the gradual decline in human lifespan, potentially alluding to the effects of sin and the cursed creation on the human body. The decreasing lifespans may symbolize the increasing distance from the original state of perfection in the Garden of Eden.

8. The flood narrative carries symbolic meanings of judgment and salvation. The floodwaters represent God's righteous judgment on sin, while the ark serves as a type (foreshadowing) of Christ, providing salvation and new beginnings for those who place their trust in God's provision.

9. The Tower of Babel represents humanity's prideful attempt to exalt themselves and make a name for themselves apart from God. The confusion of languages reflects the brokenness and disunity that results from sin and rebellion against the Creator's design and authority.

10. The call of Abram (later Abraham) and the Abrahamic Covenant introduce the concept of God's chosen people, the nation of Israel. This covenant not only promises a land and numerous descendants but also the promise of a Redeemer who will bless all nations through Abraham's lineage – a foreshadowing of the coming of Christ and the redemption of all humanity.

Exodus
BOOK SUMMARY:

Exodus, the second book of the Bible, chronicles the extraordinary deliverance of the Israelites from Egyptian bondage and their journey towards the Promised Land. This gripping narrative unveils God's mighty power and unwavering faithfulness as He rescues His chosen people from oppression, establishes His covenant with them, and prepares them for their divine destiny.

The book opens with the Israelites enduring harsh slavery in Egypt, their cries for freedom echoing through the centuries. God raises up Moses, a humble shepherd, to be their deliverer. Through a series of awe-inspiring plagues, God humbles the defiant Pharaoh and compels him to release the Israelites, setting the stage for the miraculous parting of the Red Sea and their exodus from Egypt.

As the Israelites journey through the wilderness, God's provision and protection are evident. He guides them with a pillar of cloud by day and a pillar of fire by night, sustaining them with manna from heaven and water from the rock. At Mount Sinai, God establishes His covenant with the Israelites, giving them the Ten Commandments and a system of laws to govern their nation and their relationship with Him.

The book also details the construction of the Tabernacle, a portable sanctuary where God's presence would dwell among His people. The intricate instructions for its design, furnishings, and the priesthood highlight the Israelites' need for a mediator to approach the holy God and foreshadow the ultimate sacrifice and mediation of Jesus Christ.

KEY EVENTS, CHARACTERS, AND TEACHINGS:

- The oppression of the Israelites in Egypt and the birth of Moses (Exodus 1-2)

- Moses' encounter with God at the burning bush and his call to deliver Israel (Exodus 3-4)

- The confrontation with Pharaoh and the ten plagues (Exodus 5-12)

- The Passover and the exodus from Egypt, including the miraculous parting of the Red Sea (Exodus 12-15)

- The provision of manna, water from the rock, and the battle against the Amalekites (Exodus 16-17)

- The giving of the Ten Commandments and the Mosaic Covenant at Mount Sinai (Exodus 19-24)

- The golden calf incident and Moses' intercession (Exodus 32-34)

- The instructions for the Tabernacle, its furnishings, and the priesthood (Exodus 25-31, 35-40)

EXPLORING SOME DEEPER MEANINGS:

1. The deliverance from Egypt serves as a powerful symbol of God's redemption from the bondage of sin and His ability to break the chains of oppression. The Israelites' journey represents the believer's journey from slavery to freedom, from bondage to promised inheritance.

2. The plagues that God inflicted on Egypt were not only demonstrations of His power but also judgments on the false gods worshipped by the Egyptians. Each plague exposed the impotence of these idols and affirmed God's sovereignty over all creation.

3. The Passover lamb, whose blood protected the Israelites from the final plague, foreshadows the ultimate sacrifice of Jesus Christ, the Lamb of God, whose blood provides salvation and deliverance from sin's bondage.

4. The parting of the Red Sea symbolizes God's ability to remove seemingly insurmountable obstacles and provide a way of escape for His people. It represents the believer's journey through the challenges of life, with God leading and protecting them.

5. The provision of manna and water from the rock symbolizes God's sustenance and care for His people, both physically and spiritually. It points to Jesus Christ, the Bread of Life and the Living Water, who satisfies the deepest longings of the human soul.

6. The giving of the Ten Commandments and the Mosaic Covenant established God's moral and ethical standards for His people, while also revealing their need for a Savior, as no one could perfectly keep the law.

7. The Tabernacle and its intricate design symbolize God's desire to dwell among His people and the need for a mediator to approach His holy presence. The priesthood, sacrifices, and rituals foreshadow the ultimate sacrifice of Christ and His role as the Great High Priest.

8. The golden calf incident highlights the human tendency toward idolatry and the consequences of disobedience. It also showcases God's mercy and willingness to forgive those who repent and turn back to Him.

Leviticus
BOOK SUMMARY:

Leviticus, the third book of the Bible, is a profound revelation of God's holiness and the means by which His people can maintain a consecrated relationship with Him. Given to Moses at Mount Sinai, these laws and regulations served as a blueprint for the worship, sacrificial system, and daily conduct of the Israelites, ensuring their spiritual well-being and preservation as a set-apart nation.

At the heart of Leviticus lies the intricate system of sacrifices and offerings, which provided a means for the Israelites to atone for their sins and draw near to a holy God. The book meticulously details the various types of sacrifices, such as burnt offerings, grain offerings, peace offerings, and sin offerings, each serving a specific purpose in the reconciliation process.

Leviticus also establishes the institution of the priesthood, outlining the responsibilities, qualifications, and consecration rituals for those called to minister before God. The Levites, specifically the descendants of Aaron, were entrusted with the sacred duties of offering sacrifices, maintaining the Tabernacle, and teaching the people the ways of the Lord.

Furthermore, the book sets forth principles for maintaining moral, ceremonial, and physical purity, ensuring the Israelites' separation from the pagan practices of the surrounding nations. Laws concerning clean and unclean foods, bodily discharges, and contagious diseases were given to protect the health and sanctity of the community.

Woven throughout Leviticus are profound themes of atonement, holiness, obedience, and the constant need for reconciliation with God. These themes find their ultimate fulfillment in the person and work of Jesus Christ, the perfect sacrifice and High Priest who reconciles humanity to God through His atoning death on the cross.

KEY EVENTS, CHARACTERS, AND TEACHINGS:

- Instructions for various sacrifices and offerings, including burnt, grain, peace, sin, and guilt offerings (Leviticus 1-7)

- Consecration of Aaron and his sons as priests, and the inauguration of the Tabernacle (Leviticus 8-10)

- Laws concerning clean and unclean foods, and the purification rituals after childbirth (Leviticus 11-12)

- Regulations for identifying and dealing with leprosy and other skin diseases (Leviticus 13-14)

- Instructions for the Day of Atonement, the most sacred ritual in the Israelite calendar (Leviticus 16)

- The Holiness Code, outlining moral, ceremonial, and social laws for the Israelites (Leviticus 17-26)

- Blessings for obedience and curses for disobedience (Leviticus 26)

EXPLORING SOME DEEPER MEANINGS:

As a continuation of God's redemptive plan, Leviticus offers invaluable insights into the nature of sin, the necessity of atonement, and the foreshadowing of Christ's ultimate sacrifice.

1. The intricate system of sacrifices and offerings points to the insufficiency of animal sacrifices to permanently atone for sin and the need for a perfect, once-for-all sacrifice. This is ultimately fulfilled in Jesus Christ, the Lamb of God, whose shed blood provides complete atonement and reconciliation with God.

2. The role of the high priest, who alone could enter the Most Holy Place on the Day of Atonement, foreshadows Christ's role as the Great High Priest who entered the heavenly sanctuary to make atonement for the sins of humanity.

3. The strict regulations concerning cleanliness and purity symbolize the holiness required to approach a holy God. These laws also emphasize the pervasive nature of sin and the need for purification, which is ultimately provided through the cleansing power of Christ's blood.

4. The Holiness Code (Leviticus 17-26) highlights the call for God's people to be set apart and live according to His standards of moral, ceremonial, and social purity. This foreshadows the New Testament's teachings on the believer's call to holiness and separation from the ways of the world.

5. The Sabbath and the various festivals, such as the Passover and the Feast of Tabernacles, serve as reminders of God's redemptive acts and His provision for His people. These celebrations also point to the greater spiritual realities fulfilled in Christ.

6. The blessings and curses outlined in Leviticus 26 underscore the importance of obedience to God's commands and the consequences of disobedience. Ultimately, these principles reveal humanity's inability to fully obey and the need for a Savior who can fulfill the Law's requirements.

7. The concept of the "scapegoat" (Leviticus 16:21-22), upon which the sins of the people were symbolically transferred and sent into the wilderness, foreshadows Christ's role as the sin-bearer who took upon Himself the iniquities of humanity.

Deuteronomy
BOOK SUMMARY:

Deuteronomy, the fifth book of the Bible, serves as Moses' farewell discourse to the Israelites as they stand on the cusp of entering the Promised Land of Canaan. This profound work recounts God's unwavering faithfulness, reiterates His laws and covenants, and fervently exhorts the people to remain steadfastly devoted to the Lord their God.

As its name suggests, Deuteronomy is a reiteration and expansion of the Law given at Mount Sinai, underscoring the paramount importance of obedience and the blessings that accompany it. Moses, his life nearing its end, passionately reminds the Israelites of God's mighty acts in delivering them from Egyptian bondage and His provision throughout their wilderness wanderings.

At the heart of Deuteronomy lies the renewal of the covenant between God and His chosen nation, with Moses imploring them to love the Lord wholeheartedly and to diligently teach His commandments to successive generations. The book emphasizes the exclusivity of Israel's relationship with the one true God, sternly warning against idolatry and the corrupting influences of pagan practices.

Moreover, Deuteronomy establishes the concept of the "promised land," a land flowing with milk and honey, which God has set aside as an inheritance for His obedient people. However, possession of this bountiful land is contingent upon their unwavering obedience to God's statutes and covenants.

Interwoven throughout this book are profound themes of God's faithfulness, the importance of obedience, the consequences of disobedience, and the choice between life and death, blessings and curses. These timeless truths ultimately find their fulfillment in the person and work of Jesus Christ, who perfectly embodied the Law and inaugurated a new covenant grounded in grace and faith.

KEY EVENTS, CHARACTERS, AND TEACHINGS:

- Moses' farewell addresses, recounting God's faithfulness and exhorting obedience (Deuteronomy 1-11)

- The restatement of the Ten Commandments and the Shema (Deuteronomy 5-6)

- Stern warnings against idolatry and pagan influences (Deuteronomy 7-11)

- Regulations concerning worship, civil life, and societal responsibilities (Deuteronomy 12-26)

- The blessings of obedience and the curses of disobedience (Deuteronomy 27-28)

- The renewal of the covenant and the transfer of leadership to Joshua (Deuteronomy 29-34)

EXPLORING SOME DEEPER MEANINGS:

Deuteronomy is a rich tapestry interwoven with profound spiritual truths and prophetic symbolism, beckoning readers to probe deeper into its teachings and uncover the profound foreshadowings of Christ and the New Covenant.

As the culmination of the Pentateuch, it offers invaluable insights into the very heart of God and the nature of His covenantal relationship with His people.

1. The reiteration of the Law accentuates the importance of obedience and the dire consequences of disobedience, ultimately underscoring humanity's inability to perfectly keep the Law's demands and the desperate need for a Savior who can fulfill its righteous requirements.

2. The "promised land" serves as a powerful metaphor for the believer's spiritual journey and the eternal inheritance awaiting those who remain faithful to God. It foreshadows the greater promise of everlasting life and the heavenly inheritance secured through Christ's atoning sacrifice.

3. The Shema (Deuteronomy 6:4-9), which declares the oneness of God and commands wholehearted love for Him, encapsulates the essence of true worship and devotion. This passage forms the bedrock of Jesus' teaching on the greatest commandment (Mark 12:28-31).

4. The stern warnings against idolatry and pagan influences highlight the exclusivity of Israel's relationship with God and the imperative to remain set apart from the corrupting influences of the world. This principle echoes throughout the New Testament's exhortations to separate from worldly philosophies and practices.

5. The blessings and curses delineated in Deuteronomy 27-28 underscore the inescapable consequences of obedience and disobedience, foreshadowing the spiritual axiom of reaping what is sown and the ultimate judgment and reward accompanying the choices made in this life.

6. The transfer of leadership from Moses to Joshua symbolizes the perpetuation of God's redemptive plan and the passing of the baton from one generation to the next. It foreshadows the transition from the Old Covenant to the New Covenant, with Jesus Christ as the ultimate leader and mediator.

7. The promise of a "prophet like Moses" (Deuteronomy 18:15-19) points prophetically to the coming of the Messiah, the ultimate Prophet who would speak the very words of God and lead His people into the true Promised Land of eternal life.

Joshua
BOOK SUMMARY:

The book of Joshua chronicles the remarkable story of how the Israelites, led by Joshua, conquered and occupied the Promised Land of Canaan after their exodus from Egypt. This powerful narrative showcases God's faithfulness in fulfilling His covenant promises and the obedience required of His people to claim their divine inheritance.

Following the death of Moses, God appoints Joshua as the new leader, charging him with the daunting task of leading the Israelites across the Jordan River and into the land "flowing with milk and honey." The book opens with God's assurance to Joshua, encouraging him to be strong, courageous, and unwavering in his obedience to the Law.

Through a series of miraculous events, including the parting of the Jordan River and the supernatural conquest of Jericho, God demonstrates His power and presence with His people. The Israelites are victorious in battle after battle, as long as they remain faithful to God's commands and rely on His strength.

The book also recounts the division of the Promised Land among the twelve tribes of Israel, with each tribe receiving their allotted portion as an inheritance from the Lord. Joshua's leadership is marked by his unwavering faith, his commitment to obeying God's instructions, and his determination to lead the people in destroying the pagan influences and idolatrous practices of the Canaanites.

Woven throughout the narrative are powerful themes of obedience, faith, and the fulfillment of God's promises. The book serves as a reminder that God's blessings and favor are contingent upon His people's unwavering trust and obedience to His commands.

KEY EVENTS, CHARACTERS, AND TEACHINGS:

- The commissioning of Joshua as the new leader of Israel (Joshua 1)

- The miraculous crossing of the Jordan River and the renewal of the covenant through circumcision (Joshua 2-5)

- The conquest of Jericho and the subsequent battles for the Promised Land (Joshua 6-12)

- The division of the Promised Land among the twelve tribes of Israel (Joshua 13-21)

- Joshua's farewell address and the renewal of the covenant (Joshua 23-24)

EXPLORING SOME DEEPER MEANINGS:

The book of Joshua is rich with symbolic and prophetic significance, inviting readers to invaluable insights into the nature of obedience, faith, and the fulfillment of divine promises.

1. The crossing of the Jordan River symbolizes the transition from the wilderness wanderings to the promised inheritance, echoing the believer's journey from spiritual barrenness to the abundant life in Christ.

2. The miraculous conquest of Jericho, with the walls tumbling down at the sound of trumpets and shouts, demonstrates God's power to overcome seemingly insurmountable obstacles when His people obey His commands.

3. The memorial stones taken from the Jordan River (Joshua 4:1-9) serve as a reminder to future generations of God's faithfulness and the importance of passing down the stories of His mighty acts.

4. The conquest of Canaan and the driving out of the pagan nations symbolize the spiritual battle against the forces of darkness and the need to rid oneself of idolatrous influences and worldly desires that hinder a fully devoted life to God.

5. The division of the Promised Land among the twelve tribes represents the diverse gifts and inheritances God bestows upon His people, each receiving their portion according to His sovereign plan.

6. Joshua's farewell address (Joshua 23-24) echoes the covenantal themes of Deuteronomy, calling the people to renew their commitment to God and to choose whom they will serve – a foreshadowing of the need for personal commitment and faith in the New Covenant.

7. The concept of the "cities of refuge" (Joshua 20) symbolizes the provision of safety and protection for those who seek refuge in God, foreshadowing the ultimate refuge found in Christ, the believer's stronghold and deliverer.

Numbers

BOOK SUMMARY:

The book of Numbers continues the narrative of the Israelites' journey from Egypt to the Promised Land of Canaan. Named for the two censuses taken to count the people, it chronicles the travels, challenges, and rebellions faced by the Israelites in the wilderness, as well as God's unwavering faithfulness and provision despite their disobedience.

Numbers opens with God's instructions for organizing the Israelites into tribes and companies, and the consecration of the Levites for the service of the Tabernacle. As the people set out from Mount Sinai, God's presence guides them by a pillar of cloud and fire, and His provision sustains them with manna and water from the rock.

However, the narrative shifts as the Israelites repeatedly grumble and rebel against God's leadership, leading to severe consequences, including plagues, fiery serpents, and the devastating rebellion of Korah. The book also records the tragic story of the failure of the first generation to enter the Promised Land due to their unbelief and disobedience.

Despite the people's unfaithfulness, God remains steadfast, providing laws and regulations to govern their worship, social life, and warfare. The book culminates with the new generation poised to enter Canaan, having witnessed God's judgment on the previous generation's disobedience.

KEY EVENTS, CHARACTERS, AND TEACHINGS:

- The census and organization of the Israelites (Numbers 1-4)

- The consecration of the Levites and the observance of Passover (Numbers 8-9)

- The journey from Sinai and the people's grumbling (Numbers 10-12)

- The rebellion of the spies and the judgment to wander in the wilderness (Numbers 13-14)

- Laws and regulations for offerings, purification rites, and Sabbath-keeping (Numbers 15, 18-19, 28-29)

- The rebellion of Korah, Dathan, and Abiram, and the budding of Aaron's staff (Numbers 16-17)

- The appointment of the seventy elders and the provision of quail (Numbers 11)

- The striking of the rock and Moses' sin (Numbers 20)

- The bronze serpent and the journey toward Canaan (Numbers 21)

- The story of Balaam and his talking donkey (Numbers 22-24)

- The second census and the preparation for conquering Canaan (Numbers 26-36)

EXPLORING SOME DEEPER MEANINGS:

1. The two censuses (Numbers 1 and 26) highlight the importance of accountability and the value God places on each individual within the community of faith. They also symbolize the transition from the old generation to the new, reflecting God's faithfulness to His promises across generations.

2. The Tabernacle and the consecration of the Levites (Numbers 3-4, 8) emphasize the importance of worship, service, and the need for mediators between God and His people, foreshadowing the ultimate mediation of Christ as our High Priest.

3. The pillar of cloud and fire (Numbers 9:15-23) represents God's presence, guidance, and protection over His people, symbolizing the believer's need to follow the leading of the Holy Spirit in their spiritual journey.

4. The provision of manna and water from the rock (Numbers 20:11) point to God's sustenance and His ability to provide for His people's needs, even in the midst of trials and wilderness experiences. They foreshadow Christ as the Bread of Life and the Living Water.

5. The rebellion stories (Numbers 11-12, 14, 16) underscore the consequences of disobedience, unbelief, and complaining against God's leadership. They serve as warnings against the dangers of allowing discontentment and distrust to take root in our hearts.

6. The bronze serpent (Numbers 21:4-9) foreshadows the Cross of Christ, as those who looked upon the serpent were healed, just as those who look to Christ in faith are saved from the venom of sin and death.

7. The story of Balaam and his talking donkey (Numbers 22-24) illustrates God's sovereignty over all nations and His ability to use even the most unlikely circumstances and individuals to accomplish His purposes and bless His people.

8. The laws and regulations (Numbers 15, 18-19, 28-29) emphasize the importance of holiness, obedience to God's commands, and the need for atonement and purification from sin, pointing to the ultimate sacrifice of Christ and the necessity of being cleansed by His blood.

9. The budding of Aaron's staff (Numbers 17) affirms God's choice of the Levitical priesthood and foreshadows the fruitfulness and life-giving power of Christ, the True Vine, and His ministry as our Great High Priest.

10. The appointment of the seventy elders (Numbers 11:16-30) symbolizes the distribution of God's Spirit and authority among leaders, foreshadowing the outpouring of the Holy Spirit and the empowerment of believers for ministry in the New Testament Church.

Judges
BOOK SUMMARY:

The book of Judges recounts the tumultuous period in Israel's history after the conquest of Canaan, when the people repeatedly cycled between obedience and disobedience to God, resulting in cycles of oppression and deliverance. This narrative highlights the need for godly leadership and the consequences of turning away from the Lord.

During this time, Israel had no centralized government or monarchy, and "everyone did what was right in their own eyes" (Judges 21:25). The book chronicles the exploits of various judges, or leaders, whom God raised up to deliver the Israelites from their oppressors when they cried out to Him in repentance.

These judges, such as Deborah, Gideon, Jephthah, and Samson, were anointed by God to lead the people in battle and provide temporary periods of peace and stability. However, after each judge's death, the people would once again fall into idolatry and disobedience, resulting in a cycle of oppression by neighboring nations.

The book of Judges paints a vivid picture of the depravity of human nature and the chaos that ensues when people reject God's authority and live according to their own desires. It serves as a sobering reminder of the importance of obedience to God's commands and the consequences of forsaking His ways.

KEY EVENTS, CHARACTERS, AND TEACHINGS:

- The recurring cycle of sin, oppression, repentance, and deliverance (Judges 2-16)

- The stories of the judges, including Othniel, Ehud, Deborah and Barak, Gideon, Jephthah, and Samson (Judges 3-16)

- The story of Micah's idolatry and the migration of the Danites (Judges 17-18)

- The shocking account of the Levite's concubine and the near-extinction of the tribe of Benjamin (Judges 19-21)

- The lack of a king and the statement, "everyone did what was right in their own eyes" (Judges 21:25)

EXPLORING SOME DEEPER MEANINGS:

The book of Judges uncovers profound truths about the consequences of disobedience, the need for godly leadership, and the ultimate redemption found in Christ.

1. The cyclical pattern of sin, oppression, repentance, and deliverance illustrates the human tendency toward rebellion and the need for consistent obedience to God's commands. It also highlights God's mercy and willingness to deliver those who repent and turn back to Him.

2. The judges themselves serve as both positive and negative examples of leadership. While they were initially raised up by God to deliver His people, some, like Samson, succumbed to personal weaknesses and failed to maintain their faithfulness.

3. The stories of oppression by foreign nations symbolize the spiritual oppression and bondage that result from turning away from God and embracing idolatry and sin.

4. The account of Micah's idolatry and the Danites' migration (Judges 17-18) illustrates the pervasiveness of idolatry and the human tendency to compromise spiritual principles for personal gain or convenience.

5. The shocking narrative of the Levite's concubine (Judges 19-21) exposes the depths of moral depravity and the breakdown of social order that occurs when people reject God's authority and live according to their own desires.

6. The statement "everyone did what was right in their own eyes" (Judges 21:25) underscores the need for a sovereign authority and the dangers of moral relativism and self-governance.

7. The lack of a king in Israel during this period foreshadows the need for a righteous and eternal King, ultimately fulfilled in the person and reign of Jesus Christ, the King of kings.

8. The cycles of disobedience, oppression, and deliverance point to the need for a permanent solution to the problem of sin and rebellion, which is ultimately provided through the atoning sacrifice of Christ and the establishment of His eternal kingdom.

Ruth

BOOK SUMMARY:

The book of Ruth is a heartwarming narrative set against the backdrop of the turbulent period of the Judges. It tells the story of Ruth, a Moabite woman who, after being widowed, remains loyal to her mother-in-law Naomi and follows her back to Bethlehem. This short but profound book highlights God's providence, faithfulness, and redemptive love.

The narrative begins with Naomi and her family fleeing to Moab due to famine in Bethlehem. Tragically, Naomi's husband and two sons die, leaving her and her daughters-in-law, Ruth and Orpah, as widows. While Orpah returns to her people, Ruth remains steadfastly devoted to Naomi and her God, uttering the famous words, "Where you go I will go, and where you stay I will stay. Your people will be my people and your God my God" (Ruth 1:16).

Upon their return to Bethlehem, Ruth begins gleaning in the fields of Boaz, a wealthy relative of Naomi's late husband. Boaz takes notice of Ruth's kindness and loyalty, and in accordance with the law of kinsman-redeemer, he marries her, providing for her and Naomi's future.

The book culminates with the birth of Ruth and Boaz's son, Obed, who becomes the grandfather of King David, placing Ruth in the ancestral lineage of the Messiah, Jesus Christ.

KEY EVENTS, CHARACTERS, AND TEACHINGS:

- Naomi's journey to Moab with her husband Elimelech and sons Mahlon and Kilion (Ruth 1:1-5)

- The loyalty and devotion of Ruth to Naomi, forsaking her homeland (Ruth 1:6-18)

- Ruth's gleaning in the fields of Boaz and his kindness towards her (Ruth 2)

- Naomi's plan for Ruth to seek redemption from Boaz as a kinsman-redeemer (Ruth 3)

- Boaz's redemption of Ruth and their marriage (Ruth 4:1-12)

- The birth of Obed, the grandfather of David, placing Ruth in the Messianic lineage (Ruth 4:13-22)

EXPLORING SOME DEEPER MEANINGS:

The book of Ruth is a treasured gem in Scripture, and is a narrative set during the period of the Judges, it offers a glimpse of hope and redemption amidst the darkness and chaos of that time.

1. Ruth's loyalty and devotion to Naomi, despite her status as a Moabite outsider, symbolize the inclusion of the Gentiles in God's redemptive plan and foreshadow the universality of the gospel message in the New Testament.

2. The concept of the kinsman-redeemer, embodied by Boaz, points to the ultimate role of Jesus Christ as our Redeemer, who takes on our debt and restores us to a right relationship with God.

3. The practice of gleaning (Ruth 2) highlights God's provision for the poor and marginalized, reflecting His heart for justice and care for the vulnerable.

4. The story of redemption in Ruth echoes the broader redemptive narrative of Scripture, with Boaz serving as a type of Christ, redeeming Ruth from her hopeless situation and providing her with a new identity and inheritance.

5. The inclusion of Ruth, a Moabite woman, in the genealogy of David and ultimately of Jesus Christ (Matthew 1:5) emphasizes the inclusive nature of God's redemptive plan, which transcends ethnic and cultural boundaries.

6. The theme of hesed, or steadfast love and kindness, is exemplified in the actions of Ruth, Boaz, and even Naomi, reflecting the hesed character of God Himself and His unwavering commitment to His people.

7. The birth of Obed not only secures the lineage of David and the Messiah but also symbolizes the hope of new life and the continuation of God's redemptive purposes through subsequent generations.

8. The book of Ruth serves as a beautiful picture of God's providence, weaving together seemingly disparate events and circumstances to accomplish His sovereign will and fulfill His promises.

9. The narrative's emphasis on loyalty, sacrifice, and selfless love foreshadows the ultimate sacrifice of Christ, who laid down His life for His bride, the Church.

10. The restoration of Naomi, from bitterness and emptiness to joy and fullness, reflects the transformative power of God's redemption and the hope available to all who trust in Him.

1 Samuel
BOOK SUMMARY:

The book of 1 Samuel marks a pivotal transition in the history of Israel, from the period of the Judges to the establishment of the monarchy. It chronicles the birth and life of Samuel, the last of the judges and a prominent prophet, as well as the reigns of King Saul and the anointing of David as his successor.

The narrative begins with the story of Hannah, a barren woman who pleads with God for a son. Her prayers are answered with the birth of Samuel, who is dedicated to the service of the Lord from a young age. As a prophet and judge, Samuel plays a crucial role in guiding the nation during a time of moral and spiritual decline.

As the Israelites demand a king to rule over them, God reluctantly grants their request, anointing Saul as the first king of Israel. Saul's reign is marked by both initial success and later disobedience, leading to his downfall and God's rejection of him as king.

The book then shifts its focus to David, a young shepherd boy chosen by God to be the next king. Despite facing immense challenges, including the jealousy and persecution of Saul, David's unwavering faith and trust in God ultimately lead to his victory and eventual ascension to the throne.

1 Samuel provides a rich tapestry of political, social, and spiritual narratives, highlighting the consequences of disobedience and the importance of following God's will. It also serves as a testament to God's sovereign control over history and His faithfulness to His promises.

KEY EVENTS, CHARACTERS, AND TEACHINGS:

- The birth of Samuel and his dedication to the Lord (1 Samuel 1-3)

- Samuel's ministry as a judge and prophet, and the moral decline of Israel (1 Samuel 4-7)

- The Israelites' demand for a king, and God's reluctant anointing of Saul (1 Samuel 8-10)

- Saul's reign as king, his victories and disobedience (1 Samuel 11-15)

- God's rejection of Saul and the anointing of David as the future king (1 Samuel 16)

- David's victory over Goliath and his early years in Saul's service (1 Samuel 17-20)

- David's flight from Saul's jealousy and persecution (1 Samuel 21-30)

- Saul's tragic downfall and death (1 Samuel 31)

EXPLORING SOME DEEPER MEANINGS:

1. The birth of Samuel, a child of prayer and divine promise, foreshadows the miraculous birth of Jesus Christ and God's sovereign control over history.

2. Samuel's role as a judge and prophet points to the ultimate Judge and Prophet, Jesus Christ, who would come to establish God's righteous kingdom and speak the very words of God.

3. The Israelites' demand for a king reflects humanity's desire for earthly rulers and their rejection of God's sovereign authority, a pattern that would repeat throughout history.

4. Saul's disobedience and rejection by God serve as a warning against the consequences of pride, self-reliance, and disobedience to God's commands.

5. The anointing of David as the future king symbolizes the establishment of the Davidic covenant and the promise of an eternal kingdom, ultimately fulfilled in the reign of Jesus Christ, the Son of David.

6. David's victory over Goliath demonstrates the power of faith and trust in God, even in the face of seemingly insurmountable odds, foreshadowing Christ's ultimate victory over sin and death.

7. David's persecution by Saul and his flight into the wilderness parallel the sufferings and rejection endured by Christ, the true King and Messiah.

8. The friendship between David and Jonathan exemplifies the depth of covenantal love and loyalty, reflecting the sacrificial love of Christ for His followers.

9. The recurring theme of God's sovereignty and providence throughout the narrative highlights His active involvement in human affairs and His unwavering commitment to fulfilling His promises.

10. The transition from the period of the Judges to the establishment of the monarchy sets the stage for the eventual arrival of the promised Messiah, the true King who would reign forever.

2 Samuel

BOOK SUMMARY:

The book of 2 Samuel continues the narrative from 1 Samuel, chronicling the reign of King David over the united kingdom of Israel. It is a pivotal book that portrays the triumphs and struggles of David's kingship, offering a profound exploration of faith, leadership, and the consequences of human choices.

The book begins with David's ascension to the throne after the death of Saul, and his efforts to unite the divided tribes of Israel and Judah under his rule. It then recounts David's achievements, including the capture of Jerusalem, which became the capital city, and the establishment of the Ark of the Covenant there.

However, the narrative also depicts the darker aspects of David's reign, notably his sin with Bathsheba and the subsequent consequences, including the rebellion of his son Absalom. These events serve as a poignant reminder of the frailty of human nature and the importance of repentance and restoration.

Throughout the book, the theme of God's covenant with David and the promise of an everlasting kingdom emerges. This promise finds its ultimate fulfillment in the coming of the Messiah, Jesus Christ, who is described as the "Son of David" and the heir to the eternal throne.

KEY EVENTS, CHARACTERS, AND TEACHINGS:

- David's anointing as king and his efforts to unite the tribes of Israel and Judah (2 Samuel 1-5)

- The capture of Jerusalem and the establishment of the Ark of the Covenant there (2 Samuel 5-6)

- David's victories over the Philistines and surrounding nations, expanding Israel's territory (2 Samuel 5, 8, 10)

- David's kindness to Mephibosheth, son of Jonathan (2 Samuel 9)

- David's sin with Bathsheba, the prophet Nathan's confrontation, and the consequences (2 Samuel 11-12)

- The death of David and Bathsheba's child and the birth of Solomon (2 Samuel 12)

- Amnon's sin against his sister Tamar and its consequences (2 Samuel 13)

- Absalom's rebellion against David, his death, and David's mourning (2 Samuel 13-19)

- The wise woman of Tekoa's parable to David (2 Samuel 14)

- David's census and the consequences of his disobedience (2 Samuel 24)

- The Davidic Covenant, God's promise of an everlasting kingdom through David's lineage (2 Samuel 7)

- Explorations of faith, repentance, forgiveness, and the consequences of sin and disobedience

- Foreshadowing of the coming Messiah, the "Son of David," and the fulfillment of God's covenant promises

EXPLORING SOME DEEPER MEANINGS:

1. The capture of Jerusalem and the establishment of the Ark of the Covenant there symbolized the unity of the nation under David's rule and the centralization of worship. Jerusalem became the spiritual and political capital, representing God's presence and authority.

2. David's sin with Bathsheba and the subsequent consequences demonstrate the far-reaching effects of sin, even for those in positions of leadership and authority. The narrative highlights the importance of repentance, accountability, and the need for God's forgiveness and restoration.

3. The rebellion of Absalom against David illustrates the consequences of dysfunctional family dynamics and the erosion of trust and loyalty. It also serves as a metaphor for humanity's rebellion against God's authority and the consequences of disobedience.

4. The Davidic Covenant (2 Samuel 7) is a pivotal event in the unfolding of God's redemptive plan. It establishes the promise of an everlasting kingdom through David's lineage, foreshadowing the coming of the Messiah, Jesus Christ, who would ultimately fulfill this covenant.

5. The book explores themes of faith, obedience, and the consequences of human choices. David's triumphs and failures serve as examples of the blessings that come from obedience and the consequences of disobedience, highlighting the importance of maintaining a close relationship with God.

6. The wise woman of Tekoa's parable (2 Samuel 14) demonstrates the use of wisdom and discernment in addressing complex situations and seeking reconciliation.

7. The account of David's census (2 Samuel 24) underscores the importance of trusting in God's sovereignty and provision, rather than relying on human strength and resources.

8. The narrative of Amnon's sin against Tamar and its consequences (2 Samuel 13) highlights the destructive nature of sexual sin and the importance of maintaining purity and respect within familial relationships.

9. David's kindness to Mephibosheth, son of Jonathan (2 Samuel 9), exemplifies the importance of keeping covenants and showing loyalty and mercy, even in challenging circumstances.

10. The deaths of David and Bathsheba's child and the subsequent birth of Solomon (2 Samuel 12) illustrate the consequences of sin, but also God's grace and the continuity of His covenant promises.

1 Kings
BOOK SUMMARY:

The book of 1 Kings chronicles the reigns of Israel's monarchs during a pivotal period in the nation's history. It begins with the final days of King David's life and the succession of his son, Solomon, to the throne. Under Solomon's reign, Israel experienced an era of unparalleled prosperity, wisdom, and splendor, marked by the construction of the magnificent Temple in Jerusalem.

However, the narrative takes a tragic turn as Solomon's heart is led astray by his foreign wives, leading him to compromise his devotion to God. This sets the stage for the division of the united kingdom after Solomon's death, with the northern tribes breaking away to form the kingdom of Israel under Jeroboam, while the southern tribes remained as the kingdom of Judah under Rehoboam.

The book then alternates between the parallel accounts of the northern and southern kingdoms, chronicling the reigns of various kings and their struggles with idolatry, political turmoil, and conflicts with neighboring nations. The prophets Elijah and Elisha play a prominent role, confronting the wicked kings and calling the people back to faithfulness to God.

Throughout the narrative, the author emphasizes the consequences of obedience and disobedience to God's commands, underscoring the importance of covenant faithfulness and the dire consequences of turning away from the Lord.

KEY EVENTS, CHARACTERS, AND TEACHINGS:

- The final days of King David and the succession of Solomon (1 Kings 1-2)

- Solomon's wisdom, wealth, and the construction of the Temple in Jerusalem (1 Kings 3-8)

- Solomon's downfall and the division of the kingdom (1 Kings 11-12)

- The establishment of the northern kingdom of Israel under Jeroboam and the southern kingdom of Judah under Rehoboam (1 Kings 12)

- The ministries of the prophets Elijah and Elisha, including the confrontation with Ahab and Jezebel, and the miracles they performed (1 Kings 17-22, 2 Kings 2-8)

- The reigns of various kings in Israel and Judah, their obedience or disobedience to God, and the consequences they faced (1 Kings 13-22)

- The capture and exile of the northern kingdom of Israel by the Assyrians (2 Kings 17)

- Themes of idolatry, covenant faithfulness, obedience to God's commands, and the consequences of sin and disobedience

EXPLORING SOME DEEPER MEANINGS:

1. The construction of the Temple in Jerusalem under Solomon's reign symbolized the centralization of worship and the presence of God among His people. The intricate details and grandeur of the Temple reflected the glory and majesty of the Lord.

2. Solomon's wisdom and wealth, as well as his prayer for discernment (1 Kings 3), demonstrate the blessings that come from seeking God's guidance and walking in obedience. However, his later descent into idolatry serves as a cautionary tale about the dangers of compromising one's devotion to God.

3. The division of the kingdom after Solomon's death represents the consequences of sin and disobedience, as well as the fulfillment of God's judgment prophesied earlier (1 Kings 11:11-13). It also sets the stage for the ongoing conflict between the northern and southern kingdoms.

4. The ministries of Elijah and Elisha showcase the power of God and the role of prophets in confronting sin, calling for repentance, and performing miraculous signs to authenticate their messages. Their boldness in standing against wicked rulers and false prophets exemplifies the importance of unwavering faith and obedience to God.

5. The reigns of various kings in Israel and Judah illustrate the cyclical pattern of obedience, disobedience, and the consequences that follow. The righteous kings who followed God's commands experienced blessings, while the wicked kings who embraced idolatry and disobedience faced judgment and decline.

6. The capture and exile of the northern kingdom of Israel by the Assyrians (2 Kings 17) serves as a stark reminder of the consequences of persistent disobedience and the fulfillment of God's warnings through the prophets. It also foreshadows the eventual exile of the southern kingdom of Judah due to their continued unfaithfulness.

2 Kings

<u>BOOK SUMMARY:</u>

The book of 2 Kings continues the narrative from 1 Kings, chronicling the reigns of the kings of Israel and Judah until the eventual fall and exile of both kingdoms. It serves as a sobering account of the consequences of disobedience and idolatry, while also highlighting the faithfulness of God and the unwavering ministry of His prophets.

The book begins by detailing the ministries of the prophets Elijah and Elisha, showcasing their bold confrontations with wicked kings and their powerful miracles as a testimony to the sovereignty of the Lord. It then alternates between the accounts of the northern kingdom of Israel and the southern kingdom of Judah, depicting the spiritual decline of both nations and their repeated cycles of disobedience and judgment.

Despite the warnings of the prophets and the occasional reigns of righteous kings, the people persistently turned away from God, embracing the worship of idols and adopting the corrupt practices of neighboring nations. This culminated in the conquest of the northern kingdom by the Assyrians and the eventual exile of the southern kingdom by the Babylonians, fulfilling the prophecies of God's judgment.

Throughout the narrative, the author emphasizes the importance of obedience to God's covenant and the consequences of rejecting His commands. The book also foreshadows the future restoration of a remnant and the enduring promise of God's faithfulness to His people.

<u>KEY EVENTS, CHARACTERS, AND TEACHINGS:</u>

- The ministries of Elijah and Elisha, including their miracles and confrontations with wicked rulers (2 Kings 1-8)

- The reigns of various kings in Israel and Judah, their obedience or disobedience to God, and the consequences they faced (2 Kings 9-25)

- The conquest and exile of the northern kingdom of Israel by the Assyrians (2 Kings 17)

- The reforms of King Hezekiah in Judah and the deliverance from the Assyrians (2 Kings 18-20)

- The reign of King Josiah, his rediscovery of the Book of the Law, and his efforts to restore worship (2 Kings 22-23)

- The conquest and exile of the southern kingdom of Judah by the Babylonians (2 Kings 24-25)

- The ministries of the prophets, including Isaiah, Jeremiah, and others, warning of impending judgment and calling for repentance

- Themes of idolatry, covenant faithfulness, obedience to God's commands, and the consequences of sin and disobedience

<u>EXPLORING SOME DEEPER MEANINGS:</u>

1. The miracles performed by Elijah and Elisha, such as the raising of the Shunammite's son (2 Kings 4) and the healing of Naaman the leper (2 Kings 5), demonstrate the power of God and the authenticity of His prophets' messages. These miracles served as a witness to the people, calling them to turn away from idolatry and back to the one true God.

2. The reign of King Hezekiah (2 Kings 18-20) exemplifies the blessings that come from faithfulness and obedience to God. His reforms in Judah, including the destruction of pagan idols and the restoration of worship, led to a period of revival and deliverance from the Assyrian threat, showcasing God's mercy and protection for those who trust in Him.

3. The rediscovery of the Book of the Law during the reign of King Josiah (2 Kings 22-23) highlights the importance of God's Word and the need to continually seek and obey its teachings. Josiah's reforms in response to the rediscovered Law demonstrate the transformative power of Scripture and the call to repentance and restoration.

4. The conquest and exile of the northern kingdom of Israel by the Assyrians (2 Kings 17) and the southern kingdom of Judah by the Babylonians (2 Kings 24-25) serve as a sobering fulfillment of God's warnings through the prophets. These events underscore the consequences of persistent disobedience and the reality of God's judgment on sin.

5. The ministries of the prophets, such as Isaiah and Jeremiah, played a crucial role in calling the people to repentance and warning of impending judgment. Their unwavering commitment to proclaiming God's truth, even in the face of opposition and persecution, exemplifies the importance of faithfulness and obedience to God's call.

6. The recurring cycles of obedience, disobedience, and judgment throughout the book highlight the human tendency towards sin and the need for continual repentance and renewal. These cycles also demonstrate God's patience, mercy, and willingness to restore those who turn back to Him with sincere hearts.

7. The exile and captivity of God's people serve as a turning point in the narrative, paving the way for the future restoration and the fulfillment of God's promises. The book ends with a glimmer of hope, foreshadowing the eventual return from exile and the establishment of a new covenant, setting the stage for the prophetic literature and the coming of the Messiah.

8. The interplay between the northern and southern kingdoms, their conflicts, and their spiritual decline serves as a metaphor for the division and brokenness caused by sin. It also emphasizes the importance of unity, obedience, and faithfulness to God's covenant as the path to blessing and restoration.

1 Chronicles

BOOK SUMMARY:

The book of 1 Chronicles is a historical account that provides a comprehensive genealogical record of the people of Israel, with a particular emphasis on the tribe of Judah and the lineage of King David. It serves as a bridge between the narratives of the Pentateuch and the later historical books, offering a unique perspective on the nation's history and God's covenant relationship with His chosen people.

While paralleling much of the material found in 2 Samuel, 1 Chronicles focuses on the reign of David, highlighting his preparations for the construction of the Temple and the establishment of the Levitical priesthood and worship system. The book underscores the significance of the Davidic dynasty as the lineage through which the promised Messiah would come.

1 Chronicles begins with extensive genealogies, tracing the ancestry of the Israelites from Adam to the post-exilic period. These genealogies serve as a reminder of God's faithfulness throughout generations and the continuity of His redemptive plan. The book then shifts its focus to the reign of David, chronicling his military victories, his efforts to bring the Ark of the Covenant to Jerusalem, and his preparations for the building of the Temple.

Throughout the narrative, the author emphasizes the importance of following God's commands, the centrality of worship, and the role of the Levites and priests in maintaining the proper order of worship. The book also highlights the consequences of disobedience and the blessings that come from faithfulness to God's covenant.

KEY EVENTS, CHARACTERS, AND TEACHINGS:

- Extensive genealogies from Adam to the post-exilic period (1 Chronicles 1-9)

- The reign of King David, his military victories, and the establishment of his kingdom (1 Chronicles 10-20)

- The bringing of the Ark of the Covenant to Jerusalem and the preparations for the Temple (1 Chronicles 13-17)

- The organization of the Levites and the establishment of their duties in worship and ministry (1 Chronicles 23-26)

- David's instructions to Solomon regarding the Temple construction and the need for obedience (1 Chronicles 28-29)

- The role of the priests and Levites in maintaining proper worship and religious observances

- Themes of God's covenant faithfulness, the importance of worship, obedience, and the Davidic dynasty's significance

EXPLORING SOME DEEPER MEANINGS:

1. The extensive genealogies in 1 Chronicles emphasize the continuity of God's covenant relationship with His people and the fulfillment of His promises across generations. They serve as a testament to God's faithfulness and His sovereign plan unfolding throughout history.

2. The focus on the tribe of Judah and the Davidic dynasty highlights the significance of this lineage as the promised line through which the Messiah would come. The book establishes the foundation for understanding the messianic prophecies and the fulfillment of God's redemptive plan in the New Testament.

3. The detailed accounts of David's military victories and the expansion of his kingdom underscore the theme of God's blessing and favor upon those who walk in obedience to His commands. David's successes are attributed to his trust in the Lord and his commitment to following God's ways.

4. The emphasis on the proper worship and the role of the Levites and priests reflects the importance of maintaining the sanctity of worship and adhering to God's prescribed order. The book highlights the need for reverence, obedience, and the recognition of God's holiness in all aspects of worship and religious observances.

5. The preparations for the construction of the Temple, including David's instructions to Solomon (1 Chronicles 28-29), serve as a reminder of the significance of the Temple as the dwelling place of God's presence among His people. These preparations also underscore the importance of obedience and faithfulness in undertaking tasks assigned by God.

6. The narrative of 1 Chronicles presents David as an exemplary ruler and a man after God's own heart, despite his flaws and failings. This portrayal emphasizes the grace and mercy of God, as well as the importance of repentance and a heart committed to following the Lord's ways.

7. The book's emphasis on the Levitical priesthood and the organization of worship foreshadows the establishment of the New Covenant priesthood and the role of the Church in corporate worship and ministry. It highlights the continuity of God's plan and the importance of worship and service in the lives of His people.

8. The recurring theme of obedience and its consequences throughout the book serves as a reminder of the blessings that come from faithfulness to God's commands and the consequences of disobedience. It underscores the importance of maintaining a close relationship with the Lord and aligning one's life with His will.

2 Chronicles
BOOK SUMMARY:

The book of 2 Chronicles continues the historical narrative from 1 Chronicles, focusing primarily on the united kingdom under Solomon and the subsequent divided kingdoms of Judah and Israel. Unlike the books of 1 and 2 Kings, which provide a comprehensive account of both kingdoms, 2 Chronicles concentrates mainly on the southern kingdom of Judah and the role of the Davidic dynasty in preserving the worship of the one true God.

The book opens with the reign of King Solomon, detailing his wisdom, wealth, and the construction of the magnificent Temple in Jerusalem. However, it also chronicles Solomon's eventual spiritual decline and the consequences that befell the kingdom due to his disobedience.

After the division of the kingdom, the narrative centers on the kings of Judah, highlighting the reigns of righteous rulers like Jehoshaphat, Hezekiah, and Josiah, who sought to restore proper worship and obedience to God's commands. It also emphasizes the consequences faced by wicked kings who embraced idolatry and disobedience, leading to the eventual exile of Judah to Babylon.

Throughout the book, the author emphasizes the importance of covenant faithfulness, the centrality of the Temple and its worship, and the role of the Levites and priests in maintaining the proper order of worship. The narratives also underscore the significance of repentance, prayer, and seeking the Lord, as demonstrated by the reforming kings and the revivals that followed their efforts.

KEY EVENTS, CHARACTERS, AND TEACHINGS:

- The reign of King Solomon, the construction of the Temple, and his initial wisdom and prosperity (2 Chronicles 1-9)

- The division of the kingdom and the focus on the southern kingdom of Judah (2 Chronicles 10-36)

- The reigns of righteous kings like Jehoshaphat, Hezekiah, and Josiah, their reforms, and their efforts to restore proper worship (2 Chronicles 17-20, 29-32, 34-35)

- The wicked reigns of kings who embraced idolatry and disobedience, leading to the eventual exile of Judah (2 Chronicles 33, 36)

- The ministry of the prophets, including Isaiah, Jeremiah, and others, calling for repentance and warning of impending judgment

- The role of the Levites and priests in maintaining the proper order of worship and religious observances

- The importance of prayer, repentance, and seeking the Lord, as exemplified by the reforming kings and the revivals that followed

EXPLORING SOME DEEPER MEANINGS:

1. The construction of the Temple under Solomon's reign symbolized the centralization of worship and the presence of God among His people. The intricate details and grandeur of the Temple reflected the glory and majesty of the Lord, while also serving as a reminder of the importance of obedience and reverence in worship.

2. The accounts of the righteous kings, such as Jehoshaphat, Hezekiah, and Josiah, showcase the blessings that come from faithfulness and obedience to God's commands. Their reforms and efforts to restore proper worship led to periods of spiritual revival and God's favor upon the nation, exemplifying the importance of maintaining a close relationship with the Lord.

3. The ministries of the prophets, including Isaiah and Jeremiah, played a crucial role in calling the people to repentance and warning of impending judgment. Their unwavering commitment to proclaiming God's truth, even in the face of opposition and persecution, highlights the importance of faithfulness and obedience to God's calling.

4. The repeated cycles of obedience, disobedience, and judgment throughout the book illustrate the human tendency towards sin and the need for continual repentance and renewal. These cycles also demonstrate God's patience, mercy, and willingness to restore those who turn back to Him with sincere hearts.

5. The emphasis on prayer and seeking the Lord, as exemplified by the reforming kings and the revivals that followed, underscores the importance of humility, repentance, and maintaining a posture of dependence on God. The narratives highlight the power of prayer and the blessings that come from earnestly seeking the Lord's guidance and intervention.

6. The depiction of the wicked kings who embraced idolatry and disobedience serves as a sobering reminder of the consequences of rejecting God's commands and pursuing sinful paths. The eventual exile of Judah to Babylon stands as a fulfillment of God's warnings and a testament to the reality of His judgment on persistent sin.

7. The role of the Levites and priests in maintaining the proper order of worship reflects the importance of reverence, obedience, and adhering to God's prescribed patterns in worship and religious observances. The book emphasizes the need for holiness and the recognition of God's sovereignty in all aspects of worship.

8. The focus on the Davidic dynasty and the southern kingdom of Judah highlights the continuity of God's covenant promises and the fulfillment of the messianic prophecies. The book establishes the foundation for understanding the coming of the Messiah, who would ultimately restore the kingdom and usher in an everlasting reign of righteousness.

Ezra

BOOK SUMMARY:

The book of Ezra is a historical account that chronicles the return of the Jewish exiles from Babylon to Jerusalem and the rebuilding of the Temple. It serves as a bridge between the books of Chronicles and the later prophetic works, providing a firsthand account of the fulfillment of God's promises and the restoration of His people to their homeland.

The narrative begins with the decree of King Cyrus of Persia, who allowed the Jewish exiles to return to Jerusalem and rebuild the Temple. Led by Zerubbabel and the priest Jeshua, the first wave of exiles embarked on the journey back to Judah, carrying with them the precious vessels of the Temple that had been taken during the Babylonian conquest.

Upon their arrival, the returnees faced opposition and challenges from the surrounding nations, but they remained steadfast in their commitment to rebuilding the Temple and restoring the worship of the Lord. The book details the recommencement of the sacrificial system, the observance of religious festivals, and the dedication of the newly constructed Temple.

Ezra, a skilled scribe and priest, emerges as a central figure in the latter part of the book. He led a second wave of exiles back to Jerusalem and played a pivotal role in promoting religious reforms, emphasizing the importance of adhering to the Law of Moses and maintaining the purity of the community.

Throughout the narrative, the author highlights the sovereignty of God, His faithfulness to His promises, and the importance of obedience and reverence in worship. The book serves as a testament to the power of God's redemptive work and the enduring hope of restoration for His people.

KEY EVENTS, CHARACTERS, AND TEACHINGS:

- The decree of King Cyrus and the return of the Jewish exiles from Babylon to Jerusalem (Ezra 1-2)

- The rebuilding of the Temple and the opposition faced by the returnees (Ezra 3-6)

- The ministry of Ezra the scribe and his arrival in Jerusalem (Ezra 7-8)

- Ezra's reforms and emphasis on obedience to the Law of Moses (Ezra 9-10)

- The rededication of the Temple and the restoration of worship and sacrificial system

- The observance of religious festivals and the preservation of the Jewish identity

- Themes of God's sovereignty, faithfulness to His promises, and the importance of obedience and reverence in worship

EXPLORING SOME DEEPER MEANINGS:

1. The decree of King Cyrus allowing the Jewish exiles to return to Jerusalem and rebuild the Temple (Ezra 1:1-4) marks the fulfillment of God's prophecies through Jeremiah and Isaiah, highlighting the Lord's sovereignty and His control over the events of history.

2. The opposition faced by the returnees (Ezra 4) serves as a reminder that the work of restoration and obedience to God's purposes often encounters resistance and opposition. However, the narrative emphasizes the importance of perseverance and trust in the Lord's provision and protection.

3. The rebuilding of the Temple and the restoration of worship (Ezra 3:1-7, 6:16-18) symbolize the renewal of the covenant relationship between God and His people. The Temple's reconstruction signifies the desire to reestablish the centrality of worship and the recognition of God's presence among His people.

4. Ezra's arrival and his emphasis on the study and obedience to the Law of Moses (Ezra 7:6-10) underscore the importance of maintaining the purity of worship and adhering to God's commands. The book highlights the role of spiritual leadership in guiding the community towards faithful obedience.

5. The reforms initiated by Ezra (Ezra 9-10), including the separation from foreign wives and the purification of the community, reflect the seriousness of maintaining the distinctiveness of God's people and avoiding the influence of idolatry and compromise.

6. The observance of religious festivals, such as the Passover (Ezra 6:19-22), symbolizes the renewal of the covenant relationship and the preservation of the Jewish identity. These celebrations served as reminders of God's deliverance and His faithfulness to His promises.

7. The use of genealogies and lists of names (Ezra 2, 8) emphasizes the continuity of God's covenant with His people and the importance of maintaining a record of their heritage and lineage. These lists also highlight the remnant nature of the returning exiles and their role in preserving the identity and traditions of the Jewish community.

8. The themes of obedience, repentance, and restoration throughout the book underscore the importance of maintaining a close relationship with God and aligning one's life with His commands. The narrative emphasizes the blessings that come from faithful obedience and the consequences of disobedience and compromise.

Nehemiah

The book of Nehemiah is a historical narrative that recounts the efforts of Nehemiah, the cupbearer to the Persian King Artaxerxes, in rebuilding the walls of Jerusalem and restoring the spiritual vitality of the Jewish community. It serves as a continuation of the post-exilic narrative found in the book of Ezra, chronicling the challenges and triumphs of the returned exiles as they sought to rebuild their city and reestablish their identity as God's chosen people.

The book begins with Nehemiah's distress upon learning of the desolate state of Jerusalem's walls and his fervent prayer to God for the opportunity to lead the reconstruction efforts. With the king's permission and provision, Nehemiah embarks on the arduous task of rallying the people and overcoming opposition from external enemies and internal conflicts.

Despite facing constant threats, ridicule, and opposition from those who sought to undermine the work, Nehemiah's unwavering faith and leadership enabled the completion of the wall's reconstruction in record time. This achievement not only restored the physical security of Jerusalem but also served as a powerful symbol of the people's resilience and commitment to their covenant with God.

Nehemiah's leadership extended beyond the physical reconstruction, as he initiated religious reforms, emphasizing the study of the Law, the observance of the Sabbath, and the preservation of the Jewish identity. The book concludes with the people's renewal of their covenant with God, setting the stage for the continued spiritual revival of the community.

Throughout the narrative, the author highlights the themes of prayer, perseverance, and trust in God's sovereignty, as well as the importance of obedience, repentance, and maintaining a faithful witness in the face of adversity.

KEY EVENTS, CHARACTERS, AND TEACHINGS:

- Nehemiah's distress upon learning of Jerusalem's ruined state and his prayer for God's intervention (Nehemiah 1)

- Nehemiah's journey to Jerusalem and his inspection of the ruined walls (Nehemiah 2)

- The organization and perseverance of the people in rebuilding the walls despite opposition (Nehemiah 3-4)

- The resolution of internal conflicts and the preservation of the Jewish identity (Nehemiah 5, 13)

- The dedication of the rebuilt walls and the reading of the Law by Ezra (Nehemiah 8-10)

- The observance of religious festivals and the renewal of the covenant with God (Nehemiah 9-10)

- Themes of prayer, perseverance, trust in God's sovereignty, obedience, and maintaining a faithful witness

EXPLORING SOME DEEPER MEANINGS:

1. Nehemiah's prayer for God's intervention (Nehemiah 1:4-11) exemplifies the importance of prayer and humility before the Lord. His prayer acknowledges God's sovereignty, confesses the sins of the people, and seeks divine guidance and favor for the daunting task ahead.

2. The reconstruction of the walls of Jerusalem (Nehemiah 3-4) symbolizes the rebuilding of the people's identity, security, and commitment to the covenant with God. The completion of the work, despite opposition and adversity, demonstrates the power of perseverance, unity, and trust in the Lord's provision.

3. The resolution of internal conflicts (Nehemiah 5) highlights the importance of justice, integrity, and caring for the needs of the community. Nehemiah's leadership in addressing economic disparities and exploitation exemplifies the biblical principles of compassion and social responsibility.

4. The reading of the Law by Ezra and the observance of religious festivals (Nehemiah 8-10) underscore the significance of God's Word and the renewal of the covenant relationship. These events symbolize the people's commitment to obedience, repentance, and the preservation of their spiritual identity.

5. The dedication of the rebuilt walls (Nehemiah 12) marks the culmination of the reconstruction efforts and the celebration of God's faithfulness and provision. The joy and worship expressed during this event reflect the people's gratitude and recognition of the Lord's sovereign hand in their restoration.

6. The preservation of the Jewish identity and the reforms initiated by Nehemiah (Nehemiah 13) emphasize the importance of maintaining purity, separating from compromising influences, and upholding the covenant with

God. These actions reflect the seriousness of obedience and the commitment to faithful witness.

7. The themes of prayer, perseverance, and trust in God's sovereignty throughout the book serve as reminders of the power of faith and the importance of relying on the Lord's strength and guidance in the face of adversity and opposition.

8. The narrative of Nehemiah emphasizes the importance of leadership, courage, and unwavering commitment to God's purposes. Nehemiah's example of steadfast faith, integrity, and dedication to the welfare of the community serves as a model for godly leadership and service.

Esther

BOOK SUMMARY:

The book of Esther is a remarkable narrative that chronicles the deliverance of the Jewish people from a plot of genocide orchestrated by Haman, a high-ranking official in the Persian Empire. Set during the reign of King Xerxes I, the story revolves around Esther, a young Jewish woman who becomes the queen of Persia, and her cousin Mordecai, who uncovers Haman's sinister plan.

The narrative begins with the deposition of Queen Vashti for her defiance of King Xerxes' orders. Through a series of events orchestrated by divine providence, Esther is chosen as the new queen, concealing her Jewish identity. When Mordecai refuses to bow down to Haman, the enraged official devises a scheme to annihilate all the Jews in the Persian Empire.

Risking her life, Esther courageously approaches the king, reveals her identity, and pleads for the salvation of her people. Her bravery and wisdom, combined with God's sovereign intervention, lead to the downfall of Haman and the preservation of the Jewish people. The book culminates in the establishment of the annual festival of Purim, celebrating the deliverance of the Jews and their triumph over adversity.

Throughout the narrative, the author emphasizes the themes of divine providence, courage, and the importance of maintaining one's identity and faith in the face of adversity. The book also highlights the reversal of fortunes, where the intended victims become victors, and the persecutors face the consequences of their own evil schemes.

KEY EVENTS, CHARACTERS, AND TEACHINGS:

- The deposition of Queen Vashti and the selection of Esther as the new queen (Esther 1-2)

- Mordecai's refusal to bow down to Haman and Haman's plot to annihilate the Jews (Esther 3)

- Esther's courageous approach to the king and her plea for the salvation of her people (Esther 4-5)

- The downfall of Haman and the preservation of the Jewish people (Esther 6-8)

- The establishment of the festival of Purim, celebrating the deliverance of the Jews (Esther 9-10)

- Themes of divine providence, courage, maintaining identity and faith, and the reversal of fortunes

EXPLORING SOME DEEPER MEANINGS:

1. The book of Esther does not explicitly mention God's name, but the theme of divine providence is woven throughout the narrative. The author subtly highlights how God orchestrates events and timing to protect His people, even in the most precarious situations.

2. Esther's courage and wisdom in approaching the king demonstrate the importance of taking decisive action and trusting in God's providence, even when the circumstances seem dire. Her example encourages readers to have faith and act with boldness when confronted with challenges or adversity.

3. Mordecai's refusal to bow down to Haman represents the unwavering commitment to one's faith and identity, even in the face of potential consequences. This act of defiance sets in motion the events that ultimately lead to the deliverance of the Jewish people, underscoring the significance of maintaining one's convictions.

4. The reversal of fortunes, where Haman's plot to destroy the Jews ultimately leads to his own downfall, serves as a powerful reminder of God's justice and the consequences of evil schemes. This reversal also highlights the sovereignty of God in uplifting the righteous and humbling the proud.

5. The establishment of the festival of Purim (Esther 9:20-32) symbolizes the remembrance of God's deliverance and the preservation of the Jewish identity. It serves as a perpetual celebration of the triumph of faith over adversity and the importance of passing on the legacy of God's faithfulness to future generations.

6. The character of Vashti, although brief, represents the consequences of defiance and pride. Her refusal to obey the king's command ultimately leads to her deposition, serving as a cautionary tale about the importance of humility and submission to authority.

7. The book's portrayal of Persian court life and customs provides valuable historical and cultural insights into the time period, adding depth and authenticity to the narrative while highlighting the challenges faced by the Jewish diaspora in maintaining their faith and identity in a foreign land.

Job

BOOK SUMMARY:

The book of Job is a profound exploration of the age-old question: "Why do the righteous suffer?" It is a poetic masterpiece that delves into the depths of human suffering, faith, and the sovereignty of God. The narrative revolves around Job, a righteous and prosperous man who endures unimaginable suffering, loss, and anguish, all while maintaining his integrity and trust in God.

The book opens with a celestial scene where God allows Satan to test Job's faith by inflicting devastating trials upon him. In quick succession, Job loses his wealth, his children, and his health, plunging him into a state of immense grief and despair. Three friends – Eliphaz, Bildad, and Zophar – arrive to offer comfort but end up accusing Job of hidden sin, believing his suffering is a consequence of his wrongdoing.

As the dialogue unfolds, Job steadfastly defends his innocence and questions the justice of God, grappling with the seeming paradox of a righteous life and profound suffering. A fourth friend, Elihu, attempts to mediate the discussion, offering a different perspective on God's sovereignty and the limitations of human understanding.

Ultimately, God Himself intervenes, speaking from a whirlwind and challenging Job's understanding of divine wisdom and power. Through a series of profound questions, God reveals the vastness of His creation and the limitations of human knowledge, inviting Job to trust in His sovereign and mysterious ways.

The book concludes with Job's repentance and restoration, as God blesses him with renewed prosperity and offspring.

The narrative serves as a testament to the enduring nature of faith, the complexity of human suffering, and the ultimate sovereignty and justice of God, even when His ways are beyond human comprehension.

KEY EVENTS, CHARACTERS, AND TEACHINGS:

- The prologue: Job's blameless character and prosperous life (Job 1:1-5)

- The celestial scene: God allowing Satan to test Job's faith (Job 1:6-12, 2:1-6)

- Job's devastating losses: wealth, children, and health (Job 1:13-22, 2:7-10)

- The arrival of Job's friends: Eliphaz, Bildad, and Zophar (Job 2:11-13)

- The dialogues between Job and his friends, exploring the nature of suffering and justice (Job 3-31)

- Elihu's mediation and perspective on God's sovereignty (Job 32-37)

- God's response from the whirlwind, challenging Job's understanding (Job 38-41)

- Job's repentance and restoration, with renewed blessings (Job 42)

- Themes of suffering, faith, divine sovereignty, human limitations, and the complexity of God's ways

EXPLORING SOME DEEPER MEANINGS:

1. The prologue (Job 1:1-5) establishes Job's blameless character and prosperity, setting the stage for the profound contrast with his subsequent suffering. This contrast challenges the common notion that righteousness guarantees prosperity and raises questions about the nature of suffering and divine justice.

2. The celestial scene (Job 1:6-12, 2:1-6) introduces the concept of spiritual warfare and the idea that God may allow suffering as a test of faith. It also hints at the limitations of human understanding, as the reasons for Job's trials are not initially revealed.

3. Job's lament and dialogues with his friends (Job 3-31) explore various perspectives on suffering, justice, and the nature of God. They highlight the complexity of human experience and the limitations of simplistic explanations for the mysteries of divine providence.

4. The character of Job represents the archetype of the righteous sufferer, grappling with the paradox of his suffering despite his blameless life. His unwavering faith and determination to maintain his integrity, even in the face of immense adversity, serve as a powerful example of perseverance and trust in God.

5. The speeches of Eliphaz, Bildad, and Zophar (Job 4-31) represent traditional wisdom perspectives that attempt to explain Job's suffering through conventional religious thought. Their arguments highlight the limitations of human understanding and the need for a deeper exploration of divine wisdom.

6. Elihu's mediation (Job 32-37) offers a different perspective, focusing on the sovereignty of God and the limitations of human knowledge. His speeches prepare the way for God's direct intervention, emphasizing the need for humility and trust in the face of the divine mystery.

7. God's response from the whirlwind (Job 38-41) is a profound declaration of divine wisdom, power, and sovereignty. Through a series of rhetorical questions, God challenges Job's understanding and invites him to contemplate the vastness and complexity of creation, ultimately calling for trust in the divine plan.

8. Job's repentance and restoration (Job 42) underscore the importance of humility before God and the recognition that human understanding is limited. The narrative affirms that suffering is not always a consequence of sin, and that God's ways are ultimately just, even when they are beyond human comprehension.

9. The poetic language and imagery of the book of Job add depth and richness to the exploration of profound theological themes. The vivid descriptions of nature, human emotions, and divine power evoke a sense of awe and reverence, inviting readers to ponder the mysteries of the divine and the human experience.

Psalms

BOOK SUMMARY:

The book of Psalms is a profound collection of sacred poetry that captures the depth and breadth of human emotion and spiritual experience. It is a treasury of prayers, praises, laments, and meditations, composed over a span of centuries by various authors, including King David, Asaph, the sons of Korah, and others.

The Psalms are divided into five books, each with its unique themes and literary styles. They cover a wide range of subjects, from personal struggles and corporate worship to reflections on nature, history, and the character of God. These timeless compositions express the full spectrum of human experiences, from the heights of joy and gratitude to the depths of sorrow, fear, and doubt.

At the heart of the Psalms is the intimate relationship between God and His people, a relationship that is marked by trust, praise, and a yearning for divine guidance and deliverance. The psalmists pour out their hearts to God, expressing their deepest emotions, confessing their sins, and seeking refuge in the midst of life's trials and tribulations.

The Psalms also serve as a prophetic foreshadowing of the life, ministry, and sufferings of the Messiah, Jesus Christ. Many of the Psalms contain messianic references and prophecies that find their ultimate fulfillment in the person and work of Christ.

KEY THEMES, GENRES, AND TEACHINGS:

- Praise and Worship: Exalting God's majesty, power, and faithfulness (e.g., Psalms 8, 19, 104, 148)

- Lament and Petition: Pouring out one's sorrows, fears, and pleas for God's intervention (e.g., Psalms 22, 51, 88, 130)

- Thanksgiving and Celebration: Expressing gratitude for God's blessings and deliverance (e.g., Psalms 34, 103, 116, 136)

- Wisdom and Instruction: Teachings on righteous living, the fear of the Lord, and the path to true happiness (e.g., Psalms 1, 37, 112, 119)

- Historical and Messianic Psalms: Recounting God's faithfulness in history and prophesying the coming of the Messiah (e.g., Psalms 2, 22, 110, 118)

- Imprecatory Psalms: Expressing righteous indignation and calling for God's justice (e.g., Psalms 58, 83, 109)

EXPLORING SOME DEEPER MEANINGS:

1. The Psalms offer a rich tapestry of literary devices, including parallelism, imagery, metaphors, and personification, which enhance the emotional and spiritual impact of the poetry. These literary techniques invite readers to engage with the text on a deeper level, allowing the words to resonate within their hearts and minds.

2. Many Psalms employ vivid imagery drawn from nature, such as mountains, rivers, trees, and animals, to convey spiritual truths and illustrate the majesty and power of God. These natural metaphors connect the reader to the created world and remind them of God's sovereignty over all creation.

3. The Psalms provide a profound exploration of the human condition, acknowledging the full range of emotions, from joy and praise to sorrow, anger, and doubt. The psalmists' honest expressions of their struggles and vulnerabilities offer comfort and encouragement to readers navigating their own challenges and difficulties.

4. The messianic Psalms, such as Psalms 2, 22, and 110, contain prophetic references to the coming of the Messiah, foreshadowing His suffering, resurrection, and eternal reign. These Psalms serve as a bridge between the Old and New Testaments, illuminating the continuity of God's redemptive plan.

5. The imprecatory Psalms, which express righteous indignation and call for God's justice, challenge conventional notions of forgiveness and grace. They remind readers that God is just and that there is a time for righteous anger and a call for accountability, even as mercy and forgiveness are also celebrated.

6. The wisdom Psalms, such as Psalms 1, 37, and 119, offer practical guidance for righteous living, emphasizing the fear of the Lord, obedience to God's commands, and the blessings that come from walking in His ways. These Psalms serve as a moral compass for navigating the complexities of life.

7. The use of repetition, refrains, and acrostic patterns in some Psalms (e.g., Psalms 119, 136) encourages memorization and meditation on the words, allowing the truths to permeate the reader's heart and mind more deeply.

8. The Psalms' diverse authorship, spanning different historical periods and contexts, underscores the universality of the human experience and the enduring relevance of these sacred writings. Regardless of one's circumstances, the Psalms offer a timeless source of comfort, inspiration, and guidance for all who seek to deepen their relationship with God.

Proverbs
BOOK SUMMARY:

The book of Proverbs is a remarkable collection of wisdom literature that offers practical guidance for living a righteous and successful life. Authored primarily by King Solomon, renowned for his God-given wisdom, this book imparts timeless principles and insights that transcend cultures and generations.

Proverbs is a compilation of short, memorable sayings that cover a vast array of topics, including moral character, relationships, work ethics, speech, finances, and reverence for God. These pithy statements, often expressed through vivid imagery and metaphors, are designed to shape the reader's understanding and behavior, cultivating wisdom and discernment in daily living.

At the heart of Proverbs is the fear of the Lord, which is presented as the foundation of true knowledge and understanding. The book emphasizes the importance of seeking wisdom, avoiding folly, and embracing discipline as essential components of a life well-lived.

In addition to the proverbial sayings, Proverbs also contains longer discourses and literary forms, such as parables and personifications, enriching its teachings and adding depth to its portrayal of wisdom's call.

KEY THEMES, TEACHINGS, AND LITERARY FORMS:

- The personification of wisdom as a virtuous woman, calling out to those who seek understanding (Proverbs 1:20-33, 8:1-36)

- The fear of the Lord as the beginning of knowledge and wisdom (Proverbs 1:7, 9:10)

- Practical instructions on moral character, relationships, speech, and work ethics (e.g., Proverbs 10-22)

- Warnings against folly, laziness, and the consequences of unwise choices (e.g., Proverbs 6:6-11, 26:13-16)

- Teachings on financial stewardship, generosity, and the dangers of wealth and greed (e.g., Proverbs 3:9-10, 11:24-26, 22:16)

- Parables and longer discourses on wisdom and folly (e.g., Proverbs 1-9, 24:23-34, 30:1-33, 31:10-31)

- The description of the virtuous wife and her exemplary qualities (Proverbs 31:10-31)

EXPLORING SOME DEEPER MEANINGS:

1. The personification of wisdom as a virtuous woman (Proverbs 1:20-33, 8:1-36) is a powerful literary device that portrays wisdom as a desirable and life-giving force. This metaphor invites the reader to pursue wisdom with the same passion and commitment as one would pursue a virtuous spouse.

2. The fear of the Lord, which is emphasized throughout Proverbs, is not mere dread or terror, but rather a reverent awe and submission to God's authority. It is presented as the foundation of true wisdom, acknowledging the Creator as the source of all knowledge and understanding.

3. The book's practical instructions on moral character, relationships, speech, and work ethics offer timeless principles for navigating the complexities of daily life.

These teachings promote virtues such as integrity, diligence, kindness, and self-control, which are essential for successful living and harmonious relationships.

4. The warnings against folly, laziness, and the consequences of unwise choices serve as cautionary tales, highlighting the importance of making wise decisions and avoiding the snares of temptation and complacency.

5. The teachings on financial stewardship, generosity, and the dangers of wealth and greed provide a balanced perspective on material possessions, emphasizing contentment, prudence, and the importance of using resources to honor God and bless others.

6. The longer discourses and parables found throughout Proverbs, such as the admonitions of a father to his son (Proverbs 1-9), add depth and context to the proverbial sayings, reinforcing the overarching themes of wisdom and folly.

7. The description of the virtuous wife (Proverbs 31:10-31) serves as an exemplary model of character, diligence, and wisdom. This poetic portrayal celebrates the invaluable contribution of a godly woman to her household and society, highlighting the importance of cultivating virtuous qualities in both men and women.

8. The use of vivid imagery, metaphors, and analogies throughout Proverbs adds richness and memorability to its teachings. These literary devices engage the reader's imagination and help to convey profound truths in a concise and impactful manner.

Ecclesiastes

The book of Ecclesiastes is a profound and thought-provoking philosophical exploration of the meaning of life and the ultimate purpose of human existence. Attributed to King Solomon, often referred to as the "Preacher" or "Teacher," this book stands out for its unique perspective and candid reflections on the vanities and paradoxes of life under the sun.

Ecclesiastes begins with the famous declaration, "Meaningless! Meaningless!... Utterly meaningless! Everything is meaningless" (Ecclesiastes 1:2). From this provocative opening, the author embarks on a journey to examine the various pursuits and experiences that humanity seeks for fulfillment, including wisdom, pleasure, wealth, power, and achievement.

Through a series of observations, the Preacher grapples with the apparent futility and transience of earthly endeavors, questioning the value of human toil and the ability to find lasting satisfaction apart from God. He explores the cyclical nature of life, the inevitability of death, and the limitations of human wisdom and knowledge.

However, Ecclesiastes is not merely a pessimistic lament; it also offers profound insights into the proper perspective on life and the pursuit of true meaning. The author emphasizes the importance of fearing God, living with wisdom and contentment, and enjoying the simple pleasures of life as gifts from the Creator.

Ultimately, Ecclesiastes concludes that true purpose and fulfillment can only be found in a right relationship with

God, acknowledging His sovereignty and embracing the reality that He will bring all things into judgment.

KEY THEMES, TEACHINGS, AND LITERARY FORMS:

- The vanity and futility of human pursuits and achievements apart from God (Ecclesiastes 1:2-11, 2:1-11, 12:8)

- The cyclical and repetitive nature of life, and the limitations of human wisdom and knowledge (Ecclesiastes 1:4-7, 3:1-8, 8:16-17)

- The importance of fearing God, living with wisdom, and finding contentment in the simple pleasures of life (Ecclesiastes 3:12-13, 5:18-20, 12:13-14)

- The inevitability of death and the need to make the most of one's life while on earth (Ecclesiastes 3:19-22, 9:5-6, 11:7-10)

- The use of literary devices such as poetic language, metaphors, and personal reflections to convey profound truths

EXPLORING SOME DEEPER MEANINGS:

1. The author's use of the phrase "under the sun" (Ecclesiastes 1:3, 2:18-19, 4:1) represents a limited, earthly perspective devoid of a higher, eternal purpose. It highlights the futility of pursuing meaning and satisfaction solely through earthly endeavors and temporal pursuits.

2. The descriptions of the cyclical nature of life (Ecclesiastes 1:4-7, 3:1-8) underscore the transience of human experiences and the limitations of human control over the natural order of things. These passages invite readers to consider the fleeting nature of life and the need for a higher perspective.

3. The exploration of various human pursuits, such as wisdom, pleasure, wealth, and achievement (Ecclesiastes 2:1-11), serves as a cautionary tale against finding ultimate meaning in these temporal pursuits alone. The author's candid reflections on their vanity challenge the reader to reevaluate their priorities and seek a deeper, more enduring purpose.

4. The emphasis on fearing God, living with wisdom, and finding contentment in the simple pleasures of life (Ecclesiastes 3:12-13, 5:18-20, 12:13-14) offers a counterbalance to the vanity of earthly pursuits. These passages highlight the importance of maintaining a proper perspective, embracing the gifts of God, and living with reverence and gratitude.

5. The recurring theme of the inevitability of death (Ecclesiastes 3:19-22, 9:5-6, 11:7-10) serves as a sobering reminder of the limited nature of human existence and the need to make the most of one's time on earth. These passages encourage the reader to live with purpose and make wise choices in light of their mortality.

6. The use of literary devices such as poetic language, metaphors, and personal reflections (Ecclesiastes 12:1-7) adds depth and richness to the exploration of life's complexities and the quest for meaning. These literary elements engage the reader's imagination and invite deeper contemplation of the author's insights.

7. The concluding exhortation to "fear God and keep his commandments, for this is the duty of all mankind" (Ecclesiastes 12:13) provides the ultimate resolution to the vanity and futility explored throughout the book. It affirms that true meaning and purpose can only be found in a right relationship with the Creator and obedience to His will.

Song of Solomon

BOOK SUMMARY:

The Song of Solomon, also known as the Song of Songs, is a unique and captivating love poem that celebrates the beauty and depth of romantic love between a bridegroom and his bride. This poetic masterpiece stands out in the biblical canon for its vivid imagery, sensual language, and profound exploration of the dynamics of human intimacy and desire.

The book is structured as a series of lyrical dialogues, monologues, and descriptive passages, alternating between the voices of the bride and the bridegroom. Their exchanges are rich with metaphors and symbolism, drawing parallels between their love and the splendor of nature, the allure of physical beauty, and the intensity of human passion.

While the primary theme of the Song of Solomon is romantic love, the book also carries deeper spiritual undertones. Many scholars and interpreters have understood the love between the bridegroom and the bride as a symbolic representation of the covenant relationship between God and His people, or between Christ and the Church.

The passionate language and sensual imagery challenge conventional notions of modesty and propriety, inviting readers to embrace the gift of human love and intimacy as a reflection of the divine love between God and His creation.

KEY THEMES, CHARACTERS, AND LITERARY FORMS:

- The celebration of romantic love, physical attraction, and the delights of intimacy (Song of Solomon 1:2-4, 4:9-16, 7:1-9)

- The bride and bridegroom as central characters, their mutual admiration, and their longing for union (Song of Solomon 2:8-13, 5:10-16, 8:6-7)

- The use of vivid imagery and metaphors drawn from nature, agriculture, and the natural world (Song of Solomon 2:1-3, 4:12-15, 6:11-13)

- The symbolism of the vineyard and the watchmen, potentially representing the covenant relationship and the role of spiritual leaders (Song of Solomon 1:6, 3:3-4, 8:11-12)

- The poetic structure of dialogues, monologues, and descriptive passages, creating a lyrical and sensual atmosphere

EXPLORING SOME DEEPER MEANINGS:

1. The sensual language and imagery used to describe the physical attraction and intimacy between the bride and bridegroom challenge traditional notions of propriety and modesty. These descriptions invite readers to embrace the beauty and sacredness of human love and sexuality within the context of a committed, covenantal relationship.

2. The recurring use of metaphors and similes drawn from nature, such as the comparison of the bride to a garden or vineyard (Song of Solomon 4:12-15, 8:11-12), suggests a connection between human love and the divine design of creation. These metaphors invite readers to appreciate the beauty and significance of human love as a reflection of the Creator's artistry.

3. The dialogues and monologues between the bride and bridegroom (Song of Solomon 2:8-13, 5:10-16) offer insights into the dynamics of romantic love, including the longing for union, mutual admiration, and the joy of intimacy. These passages celebrate the depth of emotional and physical connection within the context of a committed relationship.

4. The symbolism of the vineyard and the watchmen (Song of Solomon 1:6, 3:3-4, 8:11-12) has been interpreted by some scholars as representing the covenant relationship between God and His people, or between Christ and the Church. These symbolic elements invite readers to explore the spiritual dimensions of the love portrayed in the book.

5. The poetic structure, with its alternating voices and descriptive passages, creates a lyrical and sensual atmosphere that immerses the reader in the passionate expressions of love. This literary form invites readers to experience the emotions and desires portrayed in the text with heightened intensity.

6. The emphasis on the beauty and desirability of the bride and bridegroom (Song of Solomon 1:15-16, 4:1-7, 5:10-16) challenges cultural norms and celebrates the inherent worth and attractiveness of human beings as created in the image of God. These descriptions affirm the sacredness of human love and the value of physical and emotional intimacy within the context of a committed relationship.

7. The theme of longing and anticipation (Song of Solomon 2:8-13, 8:6-7) reflects the depth of emotional connection and the enduring nature of true love. These passages invite readers to appreciate the power of love to transcend time and circumstances, and to embrace the joyful anticipation of intimacy and union.

Isaiah

BOOK SUMMARY:

The book of Isaiah is a powerful prophetic masterpiece that spans the reigns of several kings in the ancient kingdom of Judah. Authored by the prophet Isaiah, it is a remarkable collection of oracles, visions, and prophecies that address the spiritual condition of God's people, confront their sins, and foretell the coming of the Messiah and the establishment of God's eternal kingdom.

Isaiah's ministry spanned a tumultuous period in Judah's history, marked by political upheavals, foreign invasions, and the ever-present threat of idolatry and apostasy. Through his prophecies, Isaiah served as a voice of warning, calling the people to repentance and faithfulness to God's covenant.

The book can be broadly divided into two main sections: chapters 1-39, often referred to as the "Book of Judgment," and chapters 40-66, known as the "Book of Consolation." The first section primarily focuses on denouncing the sins of Judah and the surrounding nations, while the latter section offers hope and comfort, foretelling the coming of the Messiah and the future restoration of God's people.

Throughout the book, Isaiah proclaims the sovereignty of God, His holiness, and His redemptive plan for humanity. The prophecies concerning the Messiah, often referred to as the "Servant Songs," provide a clear foreshadowing of the life, ministry, and sacrificial death of Jesus Christ, establishing Isaiah as a pivotal book in the unfolding of God's redemptive plan.

KEY EVENTS, CHARACTERS, AND TEACHINGS:

- Isaiah's call to prophetic ministry and his vision of God's holiness (Isaiah 6)

- Prophecies concerning the Messiah, the Suffering Servant, and the coming of God's kingdom (Isaiah 7:14, 9:6-7, 11:1-9, 53)

- Warnings and judgments against Judah, Jerusalem, and surrounding nations for their idolatry and disobedience (Isaiah 1-12, 22, 24-27, 34-35)

- Oracles of hope and comfort for God's people, foretelling their future restoration and the establishment of God's eternal kingdom (Isaiah 40-66)

- Teachings on God's sovereignty, holiness, and redemptive plan for humanity

- Calls to repentance, faithfulness, and obedience to God's covenant

EXPLORING SOME DEEPER MEANINGS:

1. The vision of God's holiness in Isaiah 6 establishes the prophet's recognition of the transcendent majesty and purity of the Lord, setting the stage for his prophetic ministry and the central theme of God's holiness throughout the book.

2. The prophecies concerning the Messiah, particularly the "Servant Songs" (Isaiah 42:1-9, 49:1-7, 50:4-9, 52:13-53:12), provide detailed and profound insights into the life, ministry, and sacrificial death of Jesus Christ. These prophecies underscore the continuity of God's redemptive plan and the fulfillment of His promises in the New Testament.

3. The warnings and judgments against Judah, Jerusalem, and surrounding nations (e.g., Isaiah 1, 5, 13-23) serve as a call to repentance and a reminder of the consequences of idolatry, injustice, and disobedience to God's commands. These prophecies emphasize the importance of maintaining covenant faithfulness and the futility of relying on human strength or alliances apart from God.

4. The oracles of hope and comfort (Isaiah 40-66) offer a powerful message of encouragement and assurance, reminding God's people of His sovereignty, His ability to redeem and restore, and the promise of a future kingdom characterized by peace, justice, and righteousness.

5. The recurring theme of God's sovereignty (Isaiah 40:12-31, 45:5-12, 46:9-11) emphasizes the Lord's supreme authority over all creation, history, and the affairs of nations. These passages invite readers to trust in God's sovereign control and to find comfort in His ability to fulfill His promises.

6. The call to repentance, faithfulness, and obedience to God's covenant (Isaiah 1:16-20, 30:15-18, 55:6-9) underscores the importance of maintaining a right relationship with the Lord and aligning one's life with His righteous standards. These exhortations remind readers of the consequences of sin and the blessings that come from walking in obedience to God's ways.

7. The vivid imagery and poetic language employed throughout the book of Isaiah (e.g., Isaiah 5:1-7, 11:6-9, 35:1-10) add depth and richness to the prophecies, engaging the reader's imagination and conveying profound truths in a powerful and memorable way.

8. The expansion of God's redemptive plan beyond the nation of Israel to include all nations (Isaiah 2:2-4, 49:6, 56:6-8) foreshadows the universal scope of the gospel message and the inclusion of the Gentiles in the kingdom of God, a theme further developed in the New Testament.

Jeremiah
BOOK SUMMARY:

The book of Jeremiah is a powerful prophetic narrative that chronicles the life and ministry of the prophet Jeremiah, who lived during the tumultuous times leading up to the Babylonian exile of Judah. Jeremiah's calling to be a "prophet to the nations" (Jeremiah 1:5) came at a young age, and his messages were often met with opposition, persecution, and rejection by the leaders and people of Judah.

Jeremiah's prophecies warned of impending judgment and called for repentance and obedience to God's covenant. He condemned the idolatry, injustice, and moral decay that had permeated Judah, and he foretold the coming destruction of Jerusalem and the Temple if the nation did not turn back to God.

Alongside these stern messages of judgment, Jeremiah also spoke words of hope and restoration, prophesying about the new covenant that God would establish with His people (Jeremiah 31:31-34). He looked ahead to a time when the exiles would return, and the Messiah would come to establish His righteous reign.

The book of Jeremiah provides a vivid portrayal of the prophet's personal life, his struggles, and his unwavering commitment to delivering God's message, even in the face of opposition and suffering. It offers profound insights into the nature of true worship, the consequences of disobedience, and the enduring faithfulness of God's love for His people.

KEY EVENTS, CHARACTERS, AND TEACHINGS:

- The call of Jeremiah as a prophet to the nations (Jeremiah 1)

- Jeremiah's confrontations with the kings and leaders of Judah (e.g., Jeremiah 22, 36)

- The symbolic acts and object lessons used by Jeremiah (e.g., the linen belt, the potter's vessel, the broken jar)

- The siege and fall of Jerusalem, the destruction of the Temple, and the Babylonian exile (Jeremiah 52)

- Jeremiah's lamentations over the devastation of Jerusalem (Lamentations)

- The prophecies of restoration and the new covenant (Jeremiah 30-33)

- The Messianic prophecies and the promise of a righteous Branch (Jeremiah 23, 33)

- Teachings on true worship, obedience, and the consequences of sin (e.g., Jeremiah 7, 17)

- The contrast between false prophets and true prophets (Jeremiah 23)

EXPLORING SOME DEEPER MEANINGS:

1. The call of Jeremiah as a prophet emphasizes God's sovereignty in choosing and equipping His servants. Jeremiah's objection of being "too young" is countered by God's assurance of His presence and authority (Jeremiah 1:6-10).

2. The symbolic acts and object lessons employed by Jeremiah (e.g., the linen belt, the potter's vessel, the broken jar) conveyed powerful messages through visual analogies, making abstract concepts more tangible and memorable.

3. The imagery of the "new covenant" (Jeremiah 31:31-34) contrasts with the old covenant, which was written on tablets of stone. The new covenant would be written on people's hearts, symbolizing a deeper, more personal relationship with God.

4. The book of Lamentations, traditionally attributed to Jeremiah, expresses the profound grief and sorrow over the destruction of Jerusalem and the Temple. Its poetic structure and vivid imagery capture the depth of suffering experienced by the people of Judah.

5. The Messianic prophecies in Jeremiah (e.g., Jeremiah 23:5-6, 33:14-16) foretell the coming of the "righteous Branch" from the line of David, who will reign with justice and righteousness, pointing to the ultimate fulfillment in Jesus Christ.

6. The contrast between false prophets and true prophets (Jeremiah 23) highlights the importance of discerning the source and truthfulness of prophetic messages. False prophets speak from their own hearts, while true prophets faithfully convey God's words.

7. The recurring theme of idolatry and the worship of false gods (e.g., Baal, the Queen of Heaven) is condemned as a violation of the exclusive covenant relationship with God. Jeremiah calls for a return to pure worship and obedience.

8. The vivid descriptions of the siege and fall of Jerusalem (Jeremiah 52) capture the devastating consequences of

Judah's disobedience and rejection of God's warnings. The destruction serves as a powerful lesson on the gravity of sin and the importance of heeding God's Word.

9. Jeremiah's personal struggles, including his lamentations and moments of doubt (e.g., Jeremiah 20:7-18), provide a candid glimpse into the emotional and spiritual challenges faced by prophets and servants of God.

10. The book of Jeremiah emphasizes the enduring faithfulness of God despite the unfaithfulness of His people. God's love and commitment to restoring and redeeming His people remain steadfast, even in the midst of judgment and exile.

Lamentations

Lamentations is a poetic masterpiece that captures the profound grief and sorrow experienced by the prophet Jeremiah and the people of Judah following the devastating destruction of Jerusalem and the Temple by the Babylonians in 586 BC. Traditionally attributed to Jeremiah, this book is a series of five laments or funeral songs, each expressing the deep anguish and mourning over the catastrophic events that befell the once-prosperous city.

Through vivid imagery, powerful metaphors, and poignant expressions of sorrow, Lamentations gives voice to the collective trauma and suffering endured by the exiled Israelites. It explores the depths of human suffering, the consequences of sin and disobedience, and the grief that accompanies the loss of cherished institutions, traditions, and ways of life.

Yet, amidst the lamentations, there are glimmers of hope and assurance in God's unfailing love, mercy, and faithfulness. The book acknowledges that the calamity was a just punishment for Judah's sins, but it also affirms the enduring nature of God's compassion and the possibility of restoration and renewal.

Lamentations is a poetic masterpiece that resonates with the human experience of grief, loss, and the struggle to find meaning and hope in the midst of profound suffering. Its raw emotions and honest expressions provide a powerful testimony to the resilience of the human spirit and the enduring presence of God's love, even in the darkest of times.

KEY EVENTS, CHARACTERS, AND TEACHINGS:

- The destruction of Jerusalem and the Temple by the Babylonians (Lamentations 1-2)

- The suffering and exile of the people of Judah (Lamentations 1-5)

- The acknowledgment of Judah's sins and the consequences of disobedience (Lamentations 1:8-9, 3:39-42)

- The lamentations of the prophet Jeremiah as an eyewitness to the devastation (Lamentations 1:1, 3:1)

- The expressions of grief, sorrow, and mourning over the loss of the city and its inhabitants (Lamentations 1-5)

- The hope and assurance in God's unfailing love, mercy, and faithfulness (Lamentations 3:22-24, 3:55-57)

- The call for repentance and restoration (Lamentations 5:21-22)

EXPLORING SOME DEEPER MEANINGS:

1. The acrostic structure of the laments, where each verse or section begins with a successive letter of the Hebrew alphabet, highlights the completeness and thoroughness of the grief expressed.

2. The personification of Jerusalem as a woman (Lamentations 1:1-12) symbolizes the profound sorrow and desolation experienced by the once-majestic city, now likened to a widow or a deserted woman.

3. The imagery of the "tears running down like a river" (Lamentations 1:16, 2:18) and the "eyes failing from weeping" (Lamentations 2:11) conveys the intensity and depth of the mourning over the calamity that befell Jerusalem.

4. The recurring metaphor of the "cup of God's wrath" (Lamentations 4:21) represents the divine judgment and punishment that Judah endured for its sins and disobedience.

5. The contrast between the former glory and prosperity of Jerusalem (Lamentations 1:6-7) and its current state of ruin and desolation (Lamentations 1:1, 4:1-2) highlights the devastating impact of sin and the consequences of turning away from God.

6. The acknowledgment of Judah's sins and the acceptance of divine punishment (Lamentations 1:8-9, 3:39-42) reflect a humility and willingness to take responsibility for their actions, paving the way for repentance and restoration.

7. The expressions of hope and assurance in God's unfailing love, mercy, and faithfulness (Lamentations 3:22-24, 3:55-57) provide a glimmer of light in the midst of deep darkness, reminding the people of God's enduring compassion and the possibility of renewal.

8. The call for repentance and restoration (Lamentations 5:21-22) invites the people to turn back to God, acknowledging their need for divine intervention and the restoration of their relationship with the Lord.

9. The vivid descriptions of the physical and emotional suffering experienced by the people of Judah (Lamentations 2:11-12, 4:3-10) serve as a powerful reminder of the horrors of war and the devastating impact of sin on human lives.

10. The laments in Lamentations resonate with the universal human experience of grief, loss, and the struggle to find meaning and purpose in the midst of profound suffering, offering a poetic expression of the depths of human emotion and the enduring presence of hope.

Ezekiel

The book of Ezekiel is a powerful prophetic narrative that records the visions, oracles, and symbolic actions of the prophet Ezekiel, who ministered to the exiles of Judah in Babylon during the sixth century BC. Ezekiel's ministry spanned a critical period in the history of Israel, spanning the fall of Jerusalem and the Temple's destruction in 586 BC, and extending into the early years of the Babylonian exile.

Ezekiel's prophecies were marked by vivid imagery, symbolic actions, and bold confrontations with the people's sin and idolatry. He warned of impending judgment on Jerusalem and called for repentance, while also offering hope for restoration and the eventual establishment of a new covenant with God.

The book is structured around Ezekiel's prophetic commissions, visions, and oracles, which often involved intricate symbolism and dramatic enactments. From the inaugural vision of God's glory (Ezekiel 1) to the detailed description of the future Temple and the restoration of Israel (Ezekiel 40-48), the book presents a rich tapestry of prophetic insights into God's sovereignty, judgment, and redemptive purposes.

Ezekiel's message emphasized the holiness of God, the consequences of sin and idolatry, and the need for individual responsibility and spiritual renewal. His visions and prophecies not only addressed the immediate circumstances of the exiles but also pointed forward to the coming of the Messiah, the establishment of the New Covenant, and the ultimate restoration of God's people in the eschaton.

KEY EVENTS, CHARACTERS, AND TEACHINGS:

- Ezekiel's inaugural vision of God's glory and his prophetic call (Ezekiel 1-3)

- The symbolic actions and object lessons (e.g., the siege of Jerusalem, the shaving of Ezekiel's head, the immobile prophet)

- The prophecies against Jerusalem, the Temple, and the nations (Ezekiel 4-24)

- The oracles against false prophets and unfaithful shepherds (Ezekiel 13, 34)

- The vision of the valley of dry bones and the promise of restoration (Ezekiel 37)

- The prophecies concerning the future Messianic kingdom and the millennial Temple (Ezekiel 40-48)

- Teachings on individual responsibility, repentance, and the need for spiritual renewal (Ezekiel 18, 33)

- The emphasis on God's holiness, sovereignty, and the vindication of His name (Ezekiel 36, 38-39)

EXPLORING SOME DEEPER MEANINGS:

1. The recurring vision of God's glory (Ezekiel 1, 10, 43) represents the manifestation of God's presence and sovereignty, even in the midst of judgment and exile.

2. The symbolic actions and object lessons (e.g., the siege of Jerusalem, the shaving of Ezekiel's head, the immobile prophet) were vivid illustrations designed to capture the attention of the exiles and convey profound spiritual truths.

3. The prophecies against Jerusalem and the Temple (Ezekiel 4-24) highlight the severity of Judah's sin and the consequences of their idolatry and disobedience, while also affirming God's justice and the inevitability of His judgment.

4. The oracles against false prophets and unfaithful shepherds (Ezekiel 13, 34) underscore the importance of spiritual leadership and the need for accountability and truthfulness in ministry.

5. The vision of the valley of dry bones (Ezekiel 37) is a powerful metaphor for the spiritual renewal and restoration of Israel, offering hope for a future revival and the fulfillment of God's promises.

6. The prophecies concerning the future Messianic kingdom and the millennial Temple (Ezekiel 40-48) provide a glimpse into the eschatological fulfillment of God's redemptive plan, with detailed descriptions of the restored Temple, the division of the land, and the worship of the Lord.

7. The teachings on individual responsibility, repentance, and spiritual renewal (Ezekiel 18, 33) emphasize the importance of personal accountability before God and the need for genuine repentance and transformation.

8. The emphasis on God's holiness, sovereignty, and the vindication of His name (Ezekiel 36, 38-39) underscores the centrality of God's glory and the ultimate purpose of His redemptive work among His people.

9. The recurring imagery of the "watchman" (Ezekiel 3, 33) highlights the prophet's role as a sentinel, warning the people of impending judgment and calling them to repentance and obedience.

10. Ezekiel's visions and prophecies often interweave elements of judgment and restoration, reflecting the tension between God's righteous judgment on sin and His unwavering commitment to redeem and restore His people according to His covenant promises.

Daniel

BOOK SUMMARY:

The book of Daniel is a powerful narrative that combines historical accounts, prophetic visions, and apocalyptic literature, providing a unique perspective on the sovereignty of God and His divine plan for the ages. Written during the Babylonian exile, the book chronicles the life and experiences of Daniel, a young Hebrew prophet who was taken captive to Babylon.

The first half of the book (chapters 1-6) recounts the historical accounts of Daniel and his three companions, Shadrach, Meshach, and Abednego, as they navigated the challenges of living in a pagan court while remaining faithful to God. These narratives showcase their unwavering devotion, miraculous deliverances, and the power of God to protect and honor those who trust in Him.

The latter half of the book (chapters 7-12) consists of apocalyptic visions and prophecies revealed to Daniel, providing insights into the future kingdoms and empires that would arise, culminating in the establishment of God's eternal kingdom. These visions offer a panoramic view of world history, with specific details concerning the Messiah, the end times, and the ultimate triumph of God's righteous rule.

Throughout the book, Daniel's life and prophecies bear witness to the sovereignty of God over the affairs of nations and individuals, challenging readers to place their trust in the eternal God who controls the course of history and the destinies of all people.

<u>KEY EVENTS, CHARACTERS, AND
TEACHINGS:</u>

- Daniel and his companions' refusal to defile themselves with the king's food (Daniel 1)

- The interpretation of Nebuchadnezzar's dreams (Daniel 2, 4)

- The deliverance of Shadrach, Meshach, and Abednego from the fiery furnace (Daniel 3)

- Daniel's interpretation of the handwriting on the wall (Daniel 5)

- Daniel's deliverance from the lions' den (Daniel 6)

- Daniel's vision of the four beasts and the Ancient of Days (Daniel 7)

- The vision of the ram and the goat (Daniel 8)

- The prophecy of the seventy weeks (Daniel 9)

- The vision of the final conflict and the end times (Daniel 10-12)

- Teachings on God's sovereignty, faithfulness, and deliverance

- Insights into future kingdoms, empires, and the coming Messiah

<u>EXPLORING SOME DEEPER MEANINGS:</u>

1. The account of Daniel and his companions refusing to defile themselves with the king's food (Daniel 1) symbolizes the importance of remaining faithful to God's commands and resisting the temptations and pressures of the world.

2. The interpretation of Nebuchadnezzar's dreams (Daniel 2, 4) showcases God's sovereignty over the affairs of nations and the future course of world empires.

3. The deliverance of Shadrach, Meshach, and Abednego from the fiery furnace (Daniel 3) demonstrates God's power to protect and deliver those who remain faithful to Him, even in the face of persecution and life-threatening situations.

4. Daniel's interpretation of the handwriting on the wall (Daniel 5) serves as a warning against pride, arrogance, and the failure to acknowledge God's sovereignty, emphasizing the importance of humility and obedience.

5. Daniel's deliverance from the lions' den (Daniel 6) highlights the power of prayer and God's ability to protect and honor those who trust in Him, even in the face of opposition and persecution.

6. The vision of the four beasts and the Ancient of Days (Daniel 7) provides a symbolic representation of the successive world empires and the eventual establishment of God's eternal kingdom, ruled by the Son of Man (a Messianic figure).

7. The vision of the ram and the goat (Daniel 8) is a prophetic foreshadowing of the conflicts between the Persian and Greek empires, with specific details concerning the rise and fall of these powers.

8. The prophecy of the seventy weeks (Daniel 9) offers a detailed timeline for the coming of the Messiah, His death, and the ultimate fulfillment of God's redemptive plan for Israel and the world.

9. The vision of the final conflict and the end times (Daniel 10-12) provides insights into the apocalyptic events leading up to the establishment of God's eternal kingdom, including the resurrection of the dead and the final judgment.

10. Throughout the book, Daniel's life and prophecies emphasize the sovereignty of God over all earthly kingdoms and rulers, challenging readers to place their trust in the eternal God who controls the course of history and the destinies of all people.

Hosea

The book of Hosea is a profound and poignant prophetic narrative that portrays God's unwavering love for His unfaithful people, Israel. Authored by the prophet Hosea during the tumultuous period of the divided kingdom, the book's central message revolves around the metaphor of God's covenant relationship with Israel being likened to a marriage.

Through Hosea's own personal experience of marrying an adulterous wife, Gomer, God provided a living illustration of His own love for the idolatrous and unfaithful nation of Israel. The book chronicles Hosea's journey of heartbreak, forgiveness, and relentless pursuit of his wayward spouse, mirroring God's unrelenting love for His people despite their spiritual adultery and apostasy.

Woven throughout the narrative are powerful prophecies of impending judgment, calls for repentance, and promises of restoration and redemption. Hosea's message served as a stern warning to the Northern Kingdom of Israel, foretelling their eventual exile and captivity at the hands of the Assyrians due to their persistent idolatry and disobedience.

Yet, amidst the harsh realities of judgment, the book offers a glimmer of hope – a promise of God's enduring love and the ultimate restoration of a covenant relationship with a remnant of His people. This hope finds its ultimate fulfillment in the New Covenant established through the sacrificial love of Jesus Christ, the Bridegroom who redeems and restores His unfaithful bride, the Church.

KEY EVENTS, CHARACTERS, AND TEACHINGS:

- Hosea's marriage to the unfaithful Gomer, and the symbolic representation of God's relationship with Israel (Hosea 1-3)

- God's indictment against Israel's idolatry and spiritual adultery (Hosea 4-7)

- Warnings of impending judgment and captivity (Hosea 8-10)

- Calls for repentance and promises of restoration (Hosea 11-14)

- Prophecies foreshadowing the coming Messiah and the New Covenant (Hosea 3, 6, 11)

EXPLORING SOME DEEPER MEANINGS:

1. Hosea's marriage to Gomer serves as a powerful metaphor for God's covenant relationship with Israel. Gomer's unfaithfulness represents Israel's spiritual adultery through idolatry, while Hosea's pursuit and restoration of his wife symbolize God's relentless love and redemptive purposes for His people.

2. The names of Hosea's children carry symbolic meanings: Jezreel ("God scatters") represents the judgment and dispersion of Israel; Lo-ruhamah ("No Mercy") signifies God's temporary withdrawal of compassion; and Lo-ammi ("Not My People") depicts Israel's rejection as God's covenant people (Hosea 1).

3. The imagery of Israel as an unfaithful wife and God as the spurned husband highlights the depth of Israel's betrayal and the intensity of God's love and jealousy for His people (Hosea 2).

4. The call for Israel to "return to the Lord" (Hosea 14:1) emphasizes the need for genuine repentance and the promise of restoration for those who turn back to God with their whole heart.

5. The prophecies concerning the Messiah and the New Covenant (Hosea 3, 6, 11) point to the ultimate fulfillment of God's redemptive plan through Jesus Christ, who would establish an everlasting covenant with His people.

6. The metaphor of the "dew" (Hosea 14:5) represents God's refreshing and reviving grace upon a repentant and restored Israel.

7. The imagery of God's love being like the "morning cloud" and "early dew" (Hosea 6:4) highlights the temporary and fleeting nature of Israel's repentance, contrasted with God's enduring faithfulness.

8. The reference to "sowing the wind and reaping the whirlwind" (Hosea 8:7) underscores the consequences of Israel's idolatry and the futility of their actions apart from God.

9. The comparison of Israel to a "trained heifer" (Hosea 10:11) symbolizes their stubbornness and resistance to God's guidance, leading to their eventual captivity and oppression.

10. The book's closing chapters (Hosea 11-14) present a poignant portrayal of God's heart torn between judgment and mercy, revealing His divine character as a loving Father who disciplines His children yet yearns to restore and bless them.

Joel

BOOK SUMMARY:

The book of Joel is a powerful prophetic oracle that calls the people of Judah to repentance and restoration in the face of a devastating locust plague and the impending "Day of the Lord." Authored by the prophet Joel, whose name means "Yahweh is God," the book is a profound message of warning, judgment, and the promise of future blessing.

The book opens with a vivid description of a catastrophic locust invasion, which serves as a metaphor for the coming judgment of God upon His people. Joel uses this natural disaster as a call to repentance, urging the people to turn back to God with fasting, weeping, and heartfelt contrition.

Beyond the immediate crisis, Joel's prophecies look ahead to the future "Day of the Lord," a time of cosmic upheaval and divine judgment upon the nations. However, in the midst of this impending judgment, Joel offers a message of hope and restoration for those who call upon the name of the Lord.

The book culminates with a promise of the outpouring of God's Spirit upon all people, a prophecy that finds its ultimate fulfillment in the events of the New Testament, particularly the Day of Pentecost (Acts 2). Joel's prophecies also envision the final judgment of the nations and the establishment of God's everlasting kingdom.

KEY EVENTS, CHARACTERS, AND TEACHINGS:

- The devastating locust plague as a metaphor for divine judgment (Joel 1)

- The call to repentance and fasting in the face of calamity (Joel 1-2)

- The prophecy of the outpouring of the Holy Spirit (Joel 2:28-32)

- The "Day of the Lord" and the final judgment (Joel 2-3)

- The restoration and blessing of Judah and Jerusalem (Joel 3)

- Teachings on repentance, the fear of the Lord, and the power of prayer

EXPLORING SOME DEEPER MEANINGS:

1. The vivid description of the locust plague (Joel 1:2-12) serves as a metaphor for the judgment and devastation that would befall Judah due to their disobedience and sin.

2. The call to repentance and fasting (Joel 1:13-20, 2:12-17) emphasizes the importance of genuine contrition and turning back to God with the whole heart, not just outward rituals.

3. The imagery of the "Day of the Lord" (Joel 2:1-11) portrays a time of cosmic upheaval and divine judgment, with references to celestial phenomena and the gathering of nations for judgment.

4. The promise of the outpouring of the Holy Spirit (Joel 2:28-32) is a significant messianic prophecy that finds its fulfillment in the events of Pentecost (Acts 2), marking the inauguration of the new covenant era.

5. The "Valley of Decision" (Joel 3:14) symbolizes the final judgment of the nations, where God will gather and judge all peoples according to their treatment of His chosen people, Israel.

6. The restoration and blessing of Judah and Jerusalem (Joel 3:18-21) envisions a time of future prosperity, security, and the establishment of God's everlasting kingdom on earth.

7. The imagery of the "latter rain" (Joel 2:23) represents the spiritual refreshing and revival that would come upon God's people through the outpouring of the Holy Spirit.

8. The reference to the "sun turning to darkness and the moon to blood" (Joel 2:31) is a symbolic depiction of the cosmic signs that will precede the great "Day of the Lord."

9. The call to "rend your heart and not your garments" (Joel 2:13) emphasizes the need for genuine, heartfelt repentance rather than mere outward displays of mourning.

10. The promise that "everyone who calls on the name of the Lord will be saved" (Joel 2:32) highlights the universal scope of God's salvation, extending beyond the confines of Israel to all who turn to Him in faith.

Amos

BOOK SUMMARY:

The book of Amos is a powerful prophetic message that thunders against social injustice, religious hypocrisy, and the complacency of God's people. Amos, a shepherd from Tekoa, was called by God to deliver a scathing rebuke to the Northern Kingdom of Israel during a time of prosperity and moral decay.

Amos's prophecies confront the sins of Israel and the surrounding nations, condemning their idolatry, oppression of the poor, and disregard for God's covenant. He boldly denounces the false sense of security and luxury that had lulled the people into spiritual complacency, warning them of impending judgment and exile.

The book opens with a series of oracles against the nations, culminating in a severe indictment against Israel and Judah. Amos uses vivid imagery and metaphors to illustrate the depth of Israel's rebellion and the certainty of God's judgment upon them.

Despite the harsh words of warning, Amos also offers a glimmer of hope – a promise of future restoration and the establishment of the Davidic kingdom under the Messiah. The book concludes with a vision of the ultimate triumph of God's sovereign plan, where His people will be planted in their land, never to be uprooted again.

KEY EVENTS, CHARACTERS, AND TEACHINGS:

- The call of Amos, a shepherd and dresser of sycamore figs (Amos 1:1, 7:14-15)

- The oracles against the nations and Israel's neighbors (Amos 1-2)

- The indictment against Israel's social injustice and religious hypocrisy (Amos 3-6)

- The visions of judgment and the inevitable exile (Amos 7-9)

- Teachings on God's justice, His sovereign choice, and the consequences of sin

- The promise of future restoration and the establishment of the Messianic kingdom (Amos 9)

EXPLORING SOME DEEPER MEANINGS:

1. The call of Amos, a shepherd and dresser of sycamore figs (Amos 1:1, 7:14-15), highlights God's sovereignty in choosing unlikely individuals to deliver His message, challenging societal norms and prejudices.

2. The oracles against the nations (Amos 1:3-2:3) demonstrate God's concern for justice and His judgment against the surrounding nations for their cruelty and oppression.

3. The indictment against Israel's social injustice (Amos 2:6-8, 5:10-15) exposes the exploitation of the poor and the perversion of justice, revealing God's anger towards those who oppress the vulnerable.

4. The condemnation of religious hypocrisy (Amos 5:21-27) challenges the superficial worship practices and empty rituals of the people, calling for genuine repentance and obedience.

5. The visions of judgment (Amos 7-9) employ powerful imagery, such as a plumb line (Amos 7:7-9) and a basket of ripe fruit (Amos 8:1-3), to symbolize the inevitability of God's judgment upon Israel.

6. The confrontation between Amos and Amaziah (Amos 7:10-17) highlights the conflict between true prophets and false religious leaders, as well as the rejection of God's message by those in power.

7. The promise of future restoration (Amos 9:11-15) envisions the rebuilding of the fallen "booth of David" and the establishment of the Messianic kingdom, where God's people will experience lasting prosperity and security.

8. The recurring phrase "the Lord roars from Zion" (Amos 1:2) emphasizes God's sovereign authority and the power of His word, which will not be silenced or ignored.

9. The imagery of the "plumb line" (Amos 7:7-9) represents God's standard of righteousness, by which the people of Israel will be measured and judged.

10. The metaphor of the "sieve" (Amos 9:9) suggests that while judgment will come upon Israel, a remnant will be preserved and restored, reflecting God's faithfulness to His covenant promises.

Obadiah

BOOK SUMMARY:

The book of Obadiah is a concise yet powerful prophetic oracle that denounces the arrogance and cruelty of Edom towards their brother nation, Israel. Obadiah, whose name means "servant of the Lord," presents a solemn message of judgment against the Edomites for their violence, pride, and lack of compassion during Jerusalem's calamity.

Despite its brevity, Obadiah's prophecy carries immense significance as it addresses the age-old conflict between the descendants of Jacob (Israel) and Esau (Edom). The book exposes Edom's treachery, their rejoicing over Judah's misfortunes, and their participation in the plundering of Jerusalem.

Obadiah's message is a stern warning against the pride, self-reliance, and complacency that led to Edom's downfall. The prophet declares that the "Day of the Lord" is imminent, a day of reckoning when God will judge the nations and vindicate His people.

While the prophecy primarily focuses on the condemnation of Edom, it also offers a glimmer of hope for the restoration of God's people and the establishment of His everlasting kingdom. Obadiah envisions a time when the righteous will possess the mountains of Esau, and the Lord's kingdom will be established forever.

KEY EVENTS, CHARACTERS, AND TEACHINGS:

- The indictment against Edom for their pride, violence, and cruelty towards Israel (Obadiah 1-9)

- The "Day of the Lord" and the judgment of Edom and the nations (Obadiah 10-16)

- The promise of the restoration of Israel and the establishment of God's kingdom (Obadiah 17-21)

- Teachings on the consequences of pride, arrogance, and lack of compassion

- The sovereignty of God in judging nations and vindicating His people

EXPLORING SOME DEEPER MEANINGS:

1. The reference to Edom as the "brother" of Israel (Obadiah 1:10, 1:12) highlights the ancient enmity between the descendants of Jacob (Israel) and Esau (Edom), emphasizing the depth of Edom's betrayal against their own kinsmen.

2. The description of Edom's pride and self-reliance (Obadiah 1:3-4) exposes their arrogance and false sense of security, which ultimately led to their downfall.

3. The imagery of Edom being brought "down to the ground" (Obadiah 1:4) symbolizes the humiliation and judgment that would befall them for their violence and cruelty towards God's people.

4. The accusation that Edom stood "at the crossroads to cut down those who were escaping" (Obadiah 1:14) portrays their lack of compassion and their active participation in the suffering of their brothers.

5. The "Day of the Lord" (Obadiah 1:15) represents the time of divine judgment, when God will punish the nations for their wickedness and vindicate His people.

6. The promise that "deliverance will come from Mount Zion" (Obadiah 1:17) points to the restoration of God's people and the establishment of His kingdom, with Jerusalem as the center of His reign.

7. The reference to the "house of Jacob" and the "house of Joseph" (Obadiah 1:18) symbolizes the reunification of the divided kingdoms of Israel and Judah under the Messianic kingdom.

8. The imagery of the "house of Esau" being consumed like "stubble" and "fire" (Obadiah 1:18) represents the complete destruction and judgment that will befall Edom.

9. The promise that "the kingdom will be the Lord's" (Obadiah 1:21) affirms God's ultimate sovereignty and the establishment of His everlasting reign over all nations.

10. The prophecy of Obadiah serves as a warning against pride, complacency, and the mistreatment of God's people, emphasizing the importance of humility, compassion, and obedience to the Lord's commands.

Jonah

The book of Jonah is a powerful narrative that chronicles the prophet Jonah's reluctant obedience to God's call and his ultimate submission to the divine will. It is a story that vividly illustrates the depth of God's compassion, His sovereignty over all nations, and His relentless pursuit of those who turn away from Him.

Jonah, commissioned by God to preach repentance to the city of Nineveh, the capital of the ruthless Assyrian empire, initially flees in the opposite direction, attempting to escape his divine mandate. His rebellion leads him into a harrowing ordeal, where he is swallowed by a great fish, symbolizing the consequences of disobedience and the need for repentance.

After being miraculously preserved and delivered from the depths, Jonah eventually obeys God's command and goes to Nineveh, where his prophetic message leads to an unexpected and widespread repentance among the people. However, Jonah's response to God's mercy towards the Ninevites reveals his own prejudice and lack of compassion, prompting a poignant lesson from God about His boundless love and concern for all people, even those considered enemies.

The book of Jonah is a profound exploration of God's sovereignty, grace, and the universal scope of His redemptive plan. It challenges readers to examine their own attitudes towards those considered "outsiders" and to embrace the boundless love and mercy of a God who desires the salvation of all nations.

KEY EVENTS, CHARACTERS, AND TEACHINGS:

- Jonah's call to preach to Nineveh and his initial rebellion (Jonah 1)

- Jonah's ordeal in the belly of the great fish (Jonah 1-2)

- Jonah's reluctant obedience and his preaching to Nineveh (Jonah 3)

- The repentance of the Ninevites and God's mercy (Jonah 3)

- Jonah's anger and God's lesson on compassion (Jonah 4)

- Teachings on obedience, repentance, and the universal scope of God's love and redemption

EXPLORING SOME DEEPER MEANINGS:

1. Jonah's flight towards Tarshish (Jonah 1:3) symbolizes his attempt to flee from the presence of God and his divine calling, highlighting the futility of running from God's sovereign will.

2. The storm and the casting of Jonah into the sea (Jonah 1:4-16) illustrate the consequences of disobedience and the impact that one person's rebellion can have on others.

3. Jonah's prayer from the belly of the fish (Jonah 2) reflects a turning point in his journey, as he acknowledges God's sovereignty and expresses a willingness to obey.

4. The repentance of the Ninevites (Jonah 3:5-9), including the king and his nobles, demonstrates the power of God's Word and the universal call to repentance, even for those considered enemies.

5. Jonah's anger towards God's mercy (Jonah 4:1-3) reveals his own prejudice and lack of compassion, contrasting with God's boundless love and concern for all people.

6. The withering of the plant that provided shade for Jonah (Jonah 4:6-11) serves as an object lesson, illustrating God's sovereignty over creation and His desire to extend mercy to those who repent, even to a great city like Nineveh.

7. The imagery of the "great fish" (Jonah 1:17, 2:10) has been interpreted as a representation of God's divine deliverance, echoing the motif of death and resurrection found throughout Scripture.

8. The book's emphasis on the universality of God's love and redemption (Jonah 4:11) challenges the exclusivist mindset and calls readers to embrace a wider perspective on God's purposes for all nations.

9. Jonah's experience of being "swallowed up" and delivered from the depths (Jonah 2:2-6) can be seen as a metaphor for the descent into death and the hope of resurrection, foreshadowing the death and resurrection of Christ.

10. The book's overarching message highlights the sovereignty of God over all nations, His willingness to extend mercy to those who repent, and His desire for obedient servants who align their hearts with His compassionate purposes.

Micah

The book of Micah is a powerful prophetic message that thunders against social injustice, religious hypocrisy, and the corruption of leadership in Judah and Israel. Micah, a contemporary of the prophet Isaiah, delivered his oracles during the reigns of Jotham, Ahaz, and Hezekiah, kings of Judah.

Micah's prophecies confront the sins of the ruling classes, the false prophets, and the spiritual complacency of the people. He denounces the exploitation of the poor, the greed of the wealthy, and the perversion of justice by those in power. With a bold and uncompromising voice, Micah calls the nation to repentance and obedience to God's commands.

While the book opens with a stern warning of impending judgment, it also offers a glimmer of hope for the remnant of God's people. Micah's famous declaration, "He has shown you, O mortal, what is good. And what does the Lord require of you? To act justly and to love mercy and to walk humbly with your God" (Micah 6:8), stands as a timeless call to godly living.

The book culminates with a vision of the future restoration of Israel and the establishment of the Messianic kingdom, where the Lord Himself will reign in peace and righteousness from Zion. Micah's prophecies foreshadow the coming of the Messiah, born in Bethlehem, who will shepherd His people and bring lasting peace and security.

KEY EVENTS, CHARACTERS, AND TEACHINGS:

- Micah's condemnation of the sins of Judah and Israel (Micah 1-3)

- The indictment against corrupt leaders, false prophets, and the exploitation of the poor (Micah 2-3)

- The call to repentance and obedience (Micah 6:1-8)

- The promise of future restoration and the establishment of the Messianic kingdom (Micah 4-5)

- The prophecy of the Messiah's birth in Bethlehem (Micah 5:2)

- Teachings on social justice, true worship, and the character of God

EXPLORING SOME DEEPER MEANINGS:

1. The opening verse, "Hear, you peoples, all of you, listen, earth and all who live in it" (Micah 1:2), establishes the universal scope of Micah's message, calling all nations to witness God's judgment and redemptive purposes.

2. The vivid imagery of mountains "melting like wax" and valleys "splitting apart" (Micah 1:4) symbolizes the upheaval and judgment that will befall Judah and Israel due to their sins.

3. Micah's condemnation of the exploitation of the poor and the seizure of lands and homes (Micah 2:1-2, 2:8-9) highlights God's concern for social justice and the protection of the vulnerable.

4. The rebuke against false prophets who "lead my people astray" (Micah 3:5) exposes the corruption of religious leadership and the danger of false teachings.

5. The rhetorical question, "Should you not embrace justice?" (Micah 3:1), challenges the people to reflect on the true essence of right living before God.

6. The promise of the "ruler over Israel" (Micah 5:2) and the prophecy of the Messiah's birth in Bethlehem point to the fulfillment of God's redemptive plan through the coming of Jesus Christ.

7. The vision of the "mountain of the Lord's temple" being established as the "highest of the mountains" (Micah 4:1-3) symbolizes the future reign of the Messiah and the universal peace that will be established under His rule.

8. The imagery of God's people "beating their swords into plowshares" (Micah 4:3) represents the transformation from war to peace and the establishment of lasting security under the Messianic kingdom.

9. Micah's declaration, "He has shown you, O mortal, what is good" (Micah 6:8), encapsulates the essence of true religion – to act justly, love mercy, and walk humbly with God.

10. The concluding promise of God's forgiveness, restoration, and faithfulness to His covenant (Micah 7:18-20) offers hope and assurance to the repentant remnant, pointing to the ultimate fulfillment of God's redemptive purposes.

Nahum
BOOK SUMMARY:

The book of Nahum is a powerful prophetic oracle that announces the impending judgment and downfall of the ancient city of Nineveh, the capital of the Assyrian Empire. Nahum, whose name means "comfort" or "consolation," delivers a message of justice and vengeance against the cruel and oppressive Assyrians.

Nineveh, known for its brutality and violence towards nations, including Israel, had become a symbol of wickedness and idolatry. Nahum's prophecies declare that the Lord is a jealous and avenging God who will not leave the guilty unpunished. The book opens with a majestic description of God's character, emphasizing His power, wrath, and sovereignty.

Through vivid imagery and poetic language, Nahum vividly portrays the destruction that awaits Nineveh. He depicts the siege, the confusion, and the ultimate demise of the once-mighty city, proclaiming that the Lord is a stronghold for those who trust in Him.

While the primary focus is on the judgment of Nineveh, Nahum's message also carries a message of hope and comfort for the people of Judah, who had suffered under Assyrian oppression. The book assures them that God will ultimately triumph over their enemies and restore their fortunes.

KEY EVENTS, CHARACTERS, AND TEACHINGS:

- The announcement of the impending judgment and fall of Nineveh (Nahum 1-3)

- The description of God's character: jealous, avenging, and sovereign (Nahum 1:2-8)

- The vivid depiction of the siege and destruction of Nineveh (Nahum 2-3)

- The proclamation of the end of Assyrian oppression and violence (Nahum 1:12-15)

- Teachings on God's justice, wrath against sin, and the protection of those who trust in Him

EXPLORING SOME DEEPER MEANINGS:

1. The opening declaration, "The Lord is a jealous and avenging God" (Nahum 1:2), establishes God's righteous anger against sin and His commitment to upholding justice.

2. The imagery of God's power over nature, such as "the mountains quake before him" and "the earth is laid waste before him" (Nahum 1:5-6), portrays His sovereign authority over all creation.

3. The rhetorical question, "Who can withstand his indignation?" (Nahum 1:6), underscores the futility of resisting God's judgment and the inevitability of His wrath upon the wicked.

4. The description of Nineveh as a "den of lions" and a "haunt of jackals" (Nahum 2:11-12) illustrates the cruelty and predatory nature of the Assyrian Empire, which preyed upon other nations.

5. The vivid imagery of the siege of Nineveh, with "the river gates are opened" and "the palace is dissolved in terror" (Nahum 2:6-7), paints a picture of the city's impending destruction.

6. The taunt, "Where is the den of the lions?" (Nahum 2:11), mocks the once-formidable power of Nineveh, now reduced to ruin and desolation.

7. The proclamation, "There is no healing for your wound" (Nahum 3:19), emphasizes the finality and completeness of Nineveh's judgment, with no hope for recovery or restoration.

8. The assurance that "The Lord is good, a stronghold in the day of trouble" (Nahum 1:7) offers comfort and hope to those who trust in God, even in the face of oppression and adversity.

9. The promise that "the wicked will no longer oppress" (Nahum 1:12) heralds the end of Assyrian tyranny and the deliverance of the oppressed nations.

10. The concluding declaration, "Your wound is incurable" (Nahum 3:19), serves as a sobering reminder of the consequences of unrepentant sin and the inevitability of God's judgment upon the wicked.

Habakkuk

BOOK SUMMARY:

The book of Habakkuk is a profound dialogue between the prophet Habakkuk and God, addressing the perplexing questions of suffering, injustice, and the apparent triumph of wickedness. Habakkuk wrestles with the reality of violence and oppression in Judah, crying out to God for intervention and deliverance.

The book opens with Habakkuk's lament, questioning God's apparent inaction in the face of the rampant evil and injustice he witnesses. God responds by revealing His sovereign plan to raise up the Babylonians as an instrument of judgment against the unfaithful nation of Judah.

Habakkuk then grapples with the seeming injustice of God using a nation even more wicked than Judah to execute His judgment. In a remarkable display of faith, Habakkuk resolves to wait patiently for God's vindication, trusting in His righteous purposes.

The book culminates with Habakkuk's powerful prayer of praise, celebrating God's majesty, power, and faithfulness. He declares his unwavering trust in the Lord, even in the midst of adversity and uncertainties, recognizing that the righteous will live by faith.

Habakkuk's message resonates with those who struggle to reconcile the existence of evil and suffering with the goodness and sovereignty of God. It offers profound insights into the nature of faith, the importance of waiting on the Lord, and the assurance that God's justice will ultimately prevail.

KEY EVENTS, CHARACTERS, AND TEACHINGS:

- Habakkuk's lament and questions about the prevalence of violence and injustice (Habakkuk 1:1-4)

- God's response and the announcement of the Babylonian invasion as judgment (Habakkuk 1:5-11)

- Habakkuk's perplexity over God's use of a wicked nation for judgment (Habakkuk 1:12-2:1)

- The famous declaration, "The righteous will live by faith" (Habakkuk 2:4)

- The five woes pronounced against the Babylonians for their wickedness (Habakkuk 2:6-20)

- Habakkuk's prayer of praise and trust in God's sovereignty and deliverance (Habakkuk 3)

EXPLORING SOME DEEPER MEANINGS:

1. Habakkuk's lament, "How long, O Lord, must I call for help?" (Habakkuk 1:2), expresses the anguish of the righteous who witness injustice and long for God's intervention.

2. God's response, "Look at the nations and watch – and be utterly amazed" (Habakkuk 1:5), reveals His sovereign plan to use even the wicked Babylonians as instruments of judgment against Judah's sins.

3. Habakkuk's perplexity, "Your eyes are too pure to look on evil; you cannot tolerate wrongdoing" (Habakkuk 1:13), highlights the tension between God's holiness and the apparent triumph of wickedness.

4. The declaration, "The righteous will live by faith" (Habakkuk 2:4), emphasizes the centrality of faith in the life of the believer, even in the face of unanswered questions and uncertainties.

5. The five woes (Habakkuk 2:6-20) pronounce judgment against the Babylonians for their greed, violence, idolatry, and exploitation, affirming God's ultimate justice and the consequences of wickedness.

6. Habakkuk's prayer in chapter 3 is a masterpiece of poetic imagery, depicting God's power, majesty, and deliverance through vivid metaphors and allusions to the Exodus and the conquest of Canaan.

7. The imagery of God's feet "trampling the sea" (Habakkuk 3:15) and His "chariots of salvation" (Habakkuk 3:8) portray His sovereign control over nature and His ability to deliver His people.

8. Habakkuk's declaration, "Yet I will rejoice in the Lord, I will be joyful in God my Savior" (Habakkuk 3:18), exemplifies unwavering trust and joy in the midst of adversity and uncertainty.

9. The reference to the "fig tree not budding" and "no herd in the stalls" (Habakkuk 3:17-18) symbolizes the potential loss of material blessings, yet Habakkuk remains steadfast in his faith.

10. The closing affirmation, "The Sovereign Lord is my strength" (Habakkuk 3:19), encapsulates the book's overarching message of finding confidence and hope in God's sovereign power and faithfulness, even when circumstances seem bleak.

Zephaniah
BOOK SUMMARY:

The book of Zephaniah is a powerful prophetic message that thunders forth God's impending judgment on Judah and the surrounding nations for their rampant idolatry, social injustice, and spiritual apostasy. Zephaniah, whose name means "the Lord hides/treasures," prophesied during the reign of King Josiah in the late 7th century BC, calling the people of Judah to urgent repentance before the coming "day of the Lord."

The book opens with a solemn announcement of God's wrath against Judah and Jerusalem, depicting a day of divine reckoning that will sweep away all life and leave utter desolation in its wake. Zephaniah condemns the corruption, violence, and complacency that had taken root in the land, warning that none would escape the Lord's judgment.

However, amid these dire warnings, Zephaniah also extends an invitation to the humble and righteous to seek the Lord and find refuge from His anger. The prophet then turns his attention to the surrounding nations, pronouncing oracles of judgment against Philistia, Moab, Ammon, Ethiopia, and Assyria for their arrogance and oppression of God's people.

Despite the severity of Judah's sin and the certainty of judgment, Zephaniah offers hope for a purified remnant who will trust in the Lord and experience His deliverance. The book culminates with a beautiful vision of future restoration, in which the Lord will gather His people, remove their reproach, and dwell among them in joyful celebration.

KEY EVENTS, CHARACTERS, AND TEACHINGS:

- The announcement of the "day of the Lord" and God's judgment on Judah and Jerusalem (Zephaniah 1:1-18)

- A call to seek humility and righteousness before the day of the Lord's anger (Zephaniah 2:1-3)

- Oracles of judgment against the surrounding nations (Philistia, Moab, Ammon, Ethiopia, Assyria) (Zephaniah 2:4-15)

- Condemnation of Jerusalem's corruption, rebellion, and disobedience (Zephaniah 3:1-7)

- The promise of a purified remnant who will trust in the Lord (Zephaniah 3:8-13)

- Prophecies of future restoration, rejoicing, and the Lord's presence among His people (Zephaniah 3:14-20)

- The concept of the "day of the Lord" as a time of judgment and reckoning

- The call to humble repentance and seeking righteousness as the pathway to deliverance

- God's universal judgment extending beyond Judah to the surrounding nations

- The preservation and purification of a faithful remnant

EXPLORING SOME DEEPER MEANINGS:

1. The concept of the "day of the Lord" as a time of judgment and reckoning, highlighting God's holiness and justice.

2. The universality of God's judgment, extending not only to Judah but also to the surrounding nations.

3. The call to humility, righteousness, and seeking the Lord as the pathway to deliverance.

4. The contrast between the corrupt leadership in Jerusalem and the faithful remnant who trust in God.

5. The symbolic language used to describe God's judgment (e.g., "a day of wrath," "a day of distress and anguish," "a day of trumpet and battle cry").

6. The promise of a restored and purified remnant, foreshadowing the future redemption of God's people.

7. The imagery of rejoicing and the Lord's presence dwelling among His people, depicting the ultimate restoration and fulfillment of God's covenant promises.

8. The messianic undertones and eschatological implications of the prophecies concerning the day of the Lord and the remnant.

9. The practical applications of repentance, humility, and seeking righteousness in light of God's impending judgment and mercy.

10. The reassurance of God's faithfulness and deliverance for those who trust in Him, even in the face of judgment and adversity.

Haggai
BOOK SUMMARY:

The book of Haggai is a powerful prophetic call to the remnant of Jews who had returned from Babylonian exile to rebuild the temple in Jerusalem. Haggai, whose name means "my feast," was a contemporary of Zechariah and delivered God's messages to the people of Judah around 520 BC, encouraging them to prioritize the reconstruction of the Lord's house.

The book opens with Haggai's rebuke of the people for neglecting the temple while focusing on their own comfortable homes. He exhorts them to consider their ways and the consequences of their misplaced priorities, which had led to economic hardship and drought. Haggai's words stir the leaders, Zerubbabel and Joshua, to lead the people in resuming the temple's reconstruction.

Through a series of four prophetic messages, Haggai reassures the people that the Lord is with them and that the glory of the new temple will surpass that of Solomon's temple. He addresses their discouragement by reminding them of God's covenant promises and the future shaking of nations when the Messiah, the "Desired of all nations," will come.

Haggai's prophecies emphasize the importance of obedience, faithfulness, and prioritizing the Lord's work, even in the face of opposition and discouragement. He calls the people to holiness and encourages them to persevere in their task, trusting in God's presence and His ultimate plan for their restoration.

KEY EVENTS, TEACHINGS, AND PROPHECIES:

- Haggai's rebuke for the people's neglect of the temple and their misplaced priorities (Haggai 1:1-11)

- The stirring of Zerubbabel and Joshua to lead the people in rebuilding the temple (Haggai 1:12-15)

- The reassurance that the Lord's presence is with the remnant (Haggai 1:13)

- The promise that the glory of the new temple will surpass that of Solomon's temple (Haggai 2:1-9)

- The prophecy of the "Desired of all nations" coming and the shaking of the nations (Haggai 2:6-9)

- The call to holiness and the promise of blessings for obedience (Haggai 2:10-19)

- The Messianic promise to Zerubbabel as the Lord's chosen servant (Haggai 2:20-23)

EXPLORING SOME DEEPER MEANINGS:

1. The importance of prioritizing the Lord's work and the reconstruction of spiritual foundations after a period of exile or spiritual drought.

2. The consequences of misplaced priorities and the neglect of God's purposes, leading to difficulties and lack of blessings.

3. The reassurance of God's presence and the encouragement to persevere in His work, even in the face of opposition or discouragement.

4. The contrast between the former glory of Solomon's temple and the promised greater glory of the new temple, potentially alluding to the coming of the Messiah.

5. The prophecy of the "Desired of all nations" and the "shaking of the nations," pointing to the future advent of Christ and the establishment of His Kingdom.

6. The emphasis on holiness, obedience, and faithfulness as prerequisites for receiving God's blessings and favor.

7. The Messianic significance of the promise to Zerubbabel as the Lord's chosen servant, foreshadowing the coming of the ultimate Messianic King.

8. The practical applications of prioritizing spiritual matters, persevering in obedience, and trusting in God's sovereign plan and timing.

9. The historical context of the post-exilic period and the challenges faced by the returning remnant in rebuilding Jerusalem and the temple.

10. The theological themes of restoration, holiness, and the fulfillment of God's covenant promises through the Messiah.

Zechariah

BOOK SUMMARY:

The book of Zechariah is a profound prophetic work that offers hope and encouragement to the remnant of Judah who had returned from Babylonian exile. Zechariah, a contemporary of Haggai, received a series of visions and oracles from the Lord, calling the people to repentance, reassuring them of God's presence, and prophesying about the coming Messiah and the restoration of Israel.

The book opens with a call to repentance, urging the people to learn from the mistakes of their ancestors and return to the Lord wholeheartedly. Zechariah then records eight night visions, which are rich in symbolism and metaphor, depicting God's plans for the protection, purification, and restoration of His people.

The central portion of the book contains two significant oracles. The first is a messianic prophecy foretelling the coming of the righteous King, who will bring peace and prosperity to Jerusalem. The second oracle addresses the shepherds and the rejection of the Good Shepherd, foreshadowing the suffering and betrayal of the Messiah.

In the latter chapters, Zechariah prophesies about the future day of the Lord, when Jerusalem will be besieged, and the Lord will go forth to battle against the nations. However, the book culminates with a glorious vision of the living waters flowing from Jerusalem, symbolizing the life-giving presence of God and the universal reign of the Lord over all nations.

KEY EVENTS, TEACHINGS, AND PROPHECIES:

- The call to repentance and the assurance of God's presence (Zechariah 1)

- The eight night visions, including the vision of the horsemen, the four horns and craftsmen, the man with a measuring line, and the cleansing of the high priest (Zechariah 1-6)

- The prophecy of the coming of the Messianic King and the removal of iniquity (Zechariah 3, 6:9-15)

- The oracle of the good and wicked shepherds, foreshadowing the rejection of the Messiah (Zechariah 11)

- The prophecy of the day of the Lord and the siege of Jerusalem (Zechariah 12-14)

- The vision of the living waters flowing from Jerusalem (Zechariah 14)

EXPLORING SOME DEEPER MEANINGS:

1. The symbolic language and imagery used in the night visions, representing God's protection, purification, and restoration of His people.

2. The messianic prophecies concerning the coming of the righteous King and the suffering of the Good Shepherd, pointing to the life, ministry, and sacrifice of Jesus Christ.

3. The concept of the day of the Lord and its implications for the future judgment and redemption of Israel and the nations.

4. The theme of repentance and the call for the people to turn away from sin and seek the Lord wholeheartedly.

5. The significance of the measuring line vision, depicting the rebuilding and expansion of Jerusalem under God's protection.

6. The cleansing of the high priest and the removal of iniquity, symbolizing the purification and restoration of spiritual leadership.

7. The oracle of the good and wicked shepherds, highlighting the consequences of rejecting God's appointed leaders and the ultimate rejection of the Messiah.

8. The prophecy of the living waters flowing from Jerusalem, representing the life-giving presence of God and the spiritual blessings that will flow from the restored city.

9. The practical applications of seeking repentance, trusting in God's protection, and embracing the Messiah as the promised King and Shepherd.

10. The historical and cultural context of the post-exilic period, shaping the messages and prophecies of Zechariah.

Zephaniah

The book of Zephaniah is a powerful prophetic work that delivers a stark message of judgment and hope to the people of Judah. Written during the reign of King Josiah (640-609 BC), Zephaniah's prophecies address the spiritual and moral decay of Judah and the surrounding nations, while also offering a glimpse of future restoration and redemption.

Zephaniah, whose name means "Yahweh has hidden" or "Yahweh has protected," was likely of royal lineage, as his genealogy is traced back four generations to King Hezekiah. This unique heritage may have given him special access and insight into the affairs of the royal court and the spiritual condition of Judah.

The book opens with a severe warning of impending judgment, known as the "Day of the Lord." This theme permeates the entire prophecy, presenting a vivid picture of God's wrath against sin and rebellion. Zephaniah's message is universal in scope, encompassing not only Judah but also the surrounding nations, emphasizing that no one can escape God's righteous judgment.

Despite the predominantly somber tone, Zephaniah's prophecy is not without hope. The final chapter shifts dramatically, offering a beautiful portrayal of restoration and renewal. God promises to purify His people, restore their fortunes, and dwell among them. This message of hope serves as a powerful reminder of God's enduring love and faithfulness, even in the face of human rebellion.

Throughout the book, Zephaniah emphasizes key theological themes such as God's sovereignty over all nations, the inevitability of divine judgment, the necessity of repentance, and the promise of ultimate restoration for the faithful remnant. His prophecies serve as both a warning and an encouragement, calling the people to turn back to God before it's too late, while assuring them of God's unfailing love and mercy for those who seek Him.

KEY EVENTS, CHARACTERS, AND TEACHINGS:

- The proclamation of the coming "Day of the Lord" as a time of judgment (Zephaniah 1:2-18)

- Warnings against idolatry, syncretism, and moral corruption in Judah (Zephaniah 1:4-6)

- Judgments pronounced against surrounding nations, including Philistia, Moab, Ammon, Ethiopia, and Assyria (Zephaniah 2:4-15)

- Specific indictments against Jerusalem for its rebellion and corruption (Zephaniah 3:1-8)

- The promise of restoration and renewal for a purified remnant (Zephaniah 3:9-20)

- The depiction of God as both a righteous judge and a loving savior

- The call to repentance and seeking the Lord (Zephaniah 2:3)

- The portrayal of God rejoicing over His people with singing (Zephaniah 3:17)

EXPLORING SOME DEEPER MEANINGS:

1. The "Day of the Lord" concept in Zephaniah is multifaceted, representing both imminent historical judgments and an ultimate eschatological event. This dual nature of prophecy highlights the cyclical pattern of judgment and redemption throughout history, culminating in God's final intervention.

2. Zephaniah's use of the phrase "I will sweep away everything from the face of the earth" (1:2) echoes the language of the flood narrative in Genesis, suggesting a cosmic reversal of creation. This imagery underscores the severity of sin and the extent of God's judgment.

3. The indictment against the "complacent" in Zephaniah 1:12 reveals a deeper spiritual issue beyond outright rebellion. It warns against spiritual apathy and the danger of presuming upon God's grace without genuine faith and obedience.

4. The judgments pronounced against the nations surrounding Judah (Zephaniah 2:4-15) demonstrate God's sovereignty over all peoples and His impartial justice. This universal scope of judgment emphasizes that no one is exempt from God's righteous standards.

5. The promise to restore "pure lips" to the people (Zephaniah 3:9) may symbolize not only the purification of speech but also the restoration of true worship and communion with God, reversing the confusion of languages at Babel.

6. The imagery of God as a warrior (Zephaniah 3:17) who then rejoices over His people with singing presents a profound picture of divine love. It transitions from judgment to restoration, highlighting the ultimate purpose of God's discipline: to bring His people back into a joyful relationship with Him.

7. The recurring theme of the "remnant" (Zephaniah 2:7, 3:12-13) emphasizes God's faithfulness in preserving a portion of His people through judgment. This concept foreshadows the New Testament idea of salvation through faith in Christ.

8. Zephaniah's call to "seek righteousness, seek humility" (2:3) as a means of potentially escaping judgment underscores the importance of both moral uprightness and a humble dependence on God, themes that resonate throughout Scripture.

9. The promise that God will "remove disaster" from His people (3:15) and "gather those who grieve" (3:18) speaks to the ultimate healing and restoration that God offers, pointing forward to the full realization of these promises in the New Jerusalem described in Revelation.

10. The book's conclusion, with its vivid imagery of God gathering, restoring, and rejoicing over His people, provides a powerful picture of divine love and the ultimate goal of redemption: an intimate, joyful relationship between God and His purified people.

Haggai
BOOK SUMMARY:

The book of Haggai is a short but potent prophetic work that addresses the post-exilic Jewish community in Jerusalem. Written in 520 BC, approximately 18 years after the first group of exiles returned from Babylon, Haggai's message focuses on the urgent need to rebuild the Temple and re-establish proper worship of Yahweh. This book provides a unique glimpse into the challenges faced by the returned exiles and God's call for spiritual renewal and obedience.

Haggai, whose name means "festal one," delivered his prophecies over a brief period of about four months. His ministry coincided with that of Zechariah, and together they played a crucial role in motivating the people to complete the reconstruction of the Temple, which had been neglected for years due to opposition and the people's focus on their own affairs.

The book is structured around four distinct messages, each precisely dated, demonstrating God's active engagement in Israel's history. Haggai's prophecies are characterized by their practical nature, addressing the immediate needs of the community while also pointing to future glory and blessing.

Throughout his messages, Haggai confronts the people's misplaced priorities, challenging them to consider their ways and redirect their efforts towards God's house. He connects the community's economic struggles and agricultural difficulties to their neglect of the Temple, emphasizing the link between spiritual obedience and material prosperity.

Haggai's prophecies also contain messianic overtones, particularly in his references to the future glory of the Temple and the coming of the "Desired of all nations." These elements provide hope and a broader perspective, encouraging the people to look beyond their immediate circumstances to God's greater plans for His people.

The book of Haggai serves as a powerful reminder of the importance of putting God first, the consequences of neglecting spiritual priorities, and the blessings that flow from obedience. It also highlights God's patience, His willingness to use human instruments to accomplish His purposes, and His faithfulness to His covenant promises.

KEY EVENTS, CHARACTERS, AND TEACHINGS:

- The call to rebuild the Temple and the people's initial response (Haggai 1:1-15)

- The promise of the Temple's future glory surpassing its former glory (Haggai 2:1-9)

- The message of blessing following obedience (Haggai 2:10-19)

- The prophecy concerning Zerubbabel, the governor of Judah (Haggai 2:20-23)

- The role of Zerubbabel (governor) and Joshua (high priest) in leading the rebuilding efforts

- The theme of misplaced priorities and the call to "consider your ways" (Haggai 1:5, 7)

- The connection between spiritual obedience and material prosperity

- The promise of God's presence with His people (Haggai 1:13, 2:4)

EXPLORING SOME DEEPER MEANINGS:

1. The precise dating of Haggai's prophecies (1:1, 2:1, 2:10, 2:20) underscores God's sovereignty over history and His active involvement in human affairs. It also lends historical credibility to the prophet's message and demonstrates the immediacy of God's word.

2. The repeated phrase "consider your ways" (1:5, 7) serves as a call to self-examination and repentance. It challenges the people to reflect on their priorities and the consequences of their choices, emphasizing personal responsibility in spiritual matters.

3. The description of the people living in "paneled houses" while God's house lies in ruins (1:4) provides a powerful metaphor for misplaced priorities. It speaks to the human tendency to prioritize personal comfort over spiritual obligations.

4. The promise that the glory of the latter house will be greater than the former (2:9) points beyond the immediate rebuilding project to a future fulfillment. This prophecy finds its ultimate realization in Christ, who brings God's presence in a way far surpassing the physical Temple.

5. The reference to shaking the heavens and the earth (2:6-7) employs apocalyptic language to describe God's intervention in history. This imagery is later echoed in the New Testament (Hebrews 12:26-28) to describe the unshakable nature of Christ's kingdom.

6. The enigmatic phrase "Desired of all nations" (2:7) has been interpreted variously as referring to the wealth of the nations or as a messianic title. In either case, it points to a future time when all nations will recognize and submit to God's rule.

7. The use of ritual purity laws as an object lesson (2:10-14) demonstrates how easily impurity spreads compared to holiness. This illustrates the insidious nature of sin and the need for intentional pursuit of holiness.

8. The promise of blessing "from this day on" (2:19) following the people's obedience highlights the immediacy of God's response to repentance and renewed commitment. It underscores the principle that obedience opens the door to divine blessing.

9. The signet ring imagery applied to Zerubbabel (2:23) recalls God's promise to David (Jeremiah 22:24-30) and points to the restoration of the Davidic line. This prophecy finds its ultimate fulfillment in Christ, the true Son of David.

10. The emphasis on the people as "the remnant" (1:12, 14; 2:2) connects Haggai's message to the broader prophetic tradition of a faithful few through whom God preserves His covenant. This concept foreshadows the New Testament church as the continuation of God's covenant people.

Zechariah
BOOK SUMMARY:

The book of Zechariah is a profound and complex prophetic work that offers a message of hope, restoration, and future glory for God's people. Written by the prophet Zechariah, whose name means "Yahweh remembers," this book was composed in the post-exilic period, beginning in 520 BC, contemporaneous with the latter part of Haggai's ministry. Zechariah's prophecies span a wide range of themes and time periods, from the immediate concerns of rebuilding the Temple to far-reaching visions of the Messianic age.

Zechariah, identified as the son of Berechiah and grandson of Iddo, was both a priest and a prophet. His dual role gave him a unique perspective on the spiritual and practical needs of the returned exiles. The book is divided into two main sections: chapters 1-8, containing a series of eight night visions and accompanying oracles, and chapters 9-14, which consist of two "burdens" or oracles concerning the future.

The first section of the book opens with a call to repentance, followed by eight symbolic visions that Zechariah received in one night. These visions, rich in apocalyptic imagery, address various aspects of God's relationship with Israel and His plans for their restoration. They include messages of comfort, warnings of judgment, and promises of future blessings. This section also includes practical instructions for the present, including the proper observance of fasts and the importance of justice and mercy.

The second section of Zechariah contains prophecies that extend far into the future, encompassing the coming of the

Messiah, the rejection and ultimate acceptance of the Messiah by Israel, and the final establishment of God's kingdom. These chapters are filled with messianic prophecies, many of which are quoted or alluded to in the New Testament as being fulfilled in Jesus Christ.

Throughout the book, Zechariah emphasizes God's sovereignty over history, His faithfulness to His covenant promises, and His plan for ultimate redemption. The prophet's message is one of encouragement to the discouraged exiles, assuring them that despite present difficulties, God has not forgotten them and has glorious plans for their future.

KEY EVENTS, CHARACTERS, AND TEACHINGS:

- The eight night visions (Zechariah 1:7-6:8), including the vision of the horsemen, the four horns and craftsmen, the man with the measuring line, Joshua the high priest, the golden lampstand, the flying scroll, the woman in a basket, and the four chariots

- The symbolic crowning of Joshua the high priest (Zechariah 6:9-15)

- Prophecies concerning the proper observance of fasts and the future transformation of fasts into feasts (Zechariah 7-8)

- The two "burdens" or oracles concerning the future (Zechariah 9-14)

- Messianic prophecies, including the coming of the king on a donkey (Zechariah 9:9), the shepherd betrayed for thirty pieces of silver (Zechariah 11:12-13), and the one pierced whom they will mourn (Zechariah 12:10)

- Prophecies of the final battle, the Lord's return, and the establishment of His kingdom (Zechariah 14)

- The recurring theme of the Lord's return to Jerusalem and His dwelling among His people

EXPLORING SOME DEEPER MEANINGS:

1. The vision of the horsemen (1:7-17) symbolizes God's awareness of world events and His commitment to restore Jerusalem. The colors of the horses may represent different aspects of divine judgment and mercy.

2. The four horns and craftsmen (1:18-21) illustrate God's judgment on the nations that scattered Israel and His provision of deliverance. This vision assures the people that their oppressors will be dealt with.

3. The man with the measuring line (2:1-13) conveys the promise of Jerusalem's future expansion and prosperity, as well as God's protective presence. The imagery of God as a "wall of fire" around the city speaks to His divine protection.

4. The vision of Joshua the high priest (3:1-10) dramatically portrays the cleansing of the priesthood and, by extension, the nation. The removal of filthy garments symbolizes the removal of sin, while the promise of the Branch points to the coming Messiah.

5. The golden lampstand and two olive trees (4:1-14) emphasize the importance of the Spirit's power in accomplishing God's purposes. This vision encourages

Zerubbabel in the task of rebuilding the Temple, assuring him of divine enablement.

6. The flying scroll (5:1-4) represents God's judgment against sin, particularly theft and false swearing. Its size, corresponding to the dimensions of the Holy Place in the Tabernacle, suggests the standard of God's holiness.

7. The woman in the basket (5:5-11) symbolizes wickedness being removed from the land, indicating a future purification of God's people.

8. The four chariots (6:1-8) represent God's judgments going out to the four corners of the earth, emphasizing His sovereignty over all nations.

9. The messianic prophecies in Zechariah find multiple fulfillments in Jesus Christ. The king riding on a donkey (9:9) is fulfilled in Christ's triumphal entry; the shepherd betrayed for thirty pieces of silver (11:12-13) is fulfilled in Judas' betrayal; and the one pierced whom they will mourn (12:10) is fulfilled in Christ's crucifixion and Israel's future recognition of Him.

10. The final chapter's vision of living waters flowing from Jerusalem (14:8) and the Lord being king over all the earth (14:9) points to the ultimate establishment of God's kingdom and the renewal of all creation. This eschatological hope provides the backdrop for understanding all of history in light of God's redemptive plan.

Malachi

BOOK SUMMARY:

The book of Malachi, the last book of the Old Testament in Christian Bibles, serves as a powerful conclusion to the prophetic literature and a bridge to the New Testament era. Written around 430 BC, approximately 100 years after the return from Babylonian exile, Malachi addresses a community that had grown complacent in their relationship with God.

The name "Malachi" means "my messenger," and whether this was the prophet's actual name or a title, it aptly describes his role in delivering God's final prophetic message before the 400-year period of silence preceding the coming of Christ.

Malachi's prophecy is structured around a series of disputes or arguments between God and His people. The prophet employs a unique question-and-answer format, presenting God's charges against the people and then voicing their anticipated objections, followed by God's responses. This rhetorical style serves to expose the hearts of the people and challenge their attitudes and behaviors.

The book addresses several key issues plaguing post-exilic Judean society, including corrupt priestly practices, unfaithfulness in marriage and divorce, social injustice, and a general spiritual apathy. Malachi calls the people to account for their half-hearted worship, their neglect of tithes and offerings, and their cynical attitude towards serving God.

Despite the strong words of rebuke, Malachi's message is ultimately one of hope and promise. The prophet points forward to the coming of the Lord, preceded by a messenger who will prepare the way. This prophecy finds its fulfillment in John the Baptist and Jesus Christ, as recognized in the New Testament.

The book concludes with a call to remember the law of Moses and a promise of the coming of Elijah before the great and dreadful day of the Lord. This ending creates a sense of anticipation and expectation, setting the stage for the events that unfold in the Gospels.

Throughout his prophecy, Malachi emphasizes God's unchanging love for His people, His desire for sincere worship and righteous living, and His promise of judgment and purification. The book serves as a timeless call to authentic faith and wholehearted devotion to God.

KEY EVENTS, CHARACTERS, AND TEACHINGS:

- God's declaration of love for Israel (Malachi 1:2-5)

- Rebuke of the priests for offering blemished sacrifices (Malachi 1:6-2:9)

- Condemnation of divorce and marital unfaithfulness (Malachi 2:10-16)

- Warning about the coming day of judgment (Malachi 2:17-3:5)

- Call to return to God through proper tithing (Malachi 3:6-12)

- Promise of blessing for the faithful remnant (Malachi 3:16-18)

- Prophecy of the coming of Elijah before the day of the Lord (Malachi 4:5-6)

- The recurring theme of God's faithfulness contrasted with the people's unfaithfulness

- Emphasis on the importance of honoring God through proper worship and ethical living

EXPLORING SOME DEEPER MEANINGS:

1. The opening declaration of God's love for Jacob over Esau (1:2-5) serves not only as a historical reference but also as a reminder of God's sovereign choice and faithfulness to His covenant promises. This sets the tone for the entire book, grounding the subsequent rebukes in the context of God's enduring love.

2. The imagery of the "table of the Lord" being defiled (1:7, 12) goes beyond mere ritual impurity. It speaks to the heart attitude behind worship, challenging believers of all times to consider the quality and sincerity of their devotion to God.

3. The condemnation of the priests (2:1-9) for failing to honor God and teach truth highlights the critical role of spiritual leaders. Their influence, for good or ill, impacts the entire community, emphasizing the weighty responsibility of those in spiritual authority.

4. Malachi's strong words against divorce (2:13-16) not only address a social issue of his time but also reveal God's heart for the sanctity of marriage. The prophet connects marital faithfulness to spiritual faithfulness, viewing both as reflections of one's covenant relationship with God.

5. The concept of the Lord coming to His temple "suddenly" (3:1) carries dual prophetic significance. It points to both the first coming of Christ and His future return, emphasizing the need for constant spiritual readiness.

6. The vivid imagery of the refiner's fire and launderer's soap (3:2-3) illustrates the purifying nature of God's judgment. This purification process, while potentially painful, is ultimately redemptive, aimed at producing a people fit for true worship.

7. The call to "test" God in the matter of tithing (3:10) is a unique invitation in Scripture. It demonstrates God's desire for His people to experience His faithfulness firsthand, challenging them to trust Him in practical areas of life.

8. The description of a "book of remembrance" for those who fear the Lord (3:16) offers comfort to the faithful remnant. It assures them that their devotion to God, even in difficult times, is not overlooked but is precious in His sight.

9. The promise of the "sun of righteousness" rising with healing in its wings (4:2) is a beautiful messianic metaphor. It points to the coming of Christ, who brings light, healing, and restoration to a world darkened by sin.

10. The final prophecy concerning the coming of Elijah (4:5-6) creates a bridge between the Old and New Testaments. Fulfilled in the ministry of John the Baptist, it emphasizes the preparatory nature of repentance in receiving God's kingdom.

Matthew

BOOK SUMMARY:

The Gospel of Matthew, traditionally attributed to the apostle Matthew (also known as Levi), is the first book of the New Testament and serves as a bridge between the Old and New Covenants. Written primarily for a Jewish audience, Matthew's account presents Jesus as the long-awaited Messiah and the fulfillment of Old Testament prophecies. The book was likely composed between 70-80 AD, after the destruction of the Jerusalem Temple.

Matthew's Gospel is structured around five major discourses of Jesus, interspersed with narrative sections detailing His life, ministry, death, and resurrection. This structure is reminiscent of the five books of the Torah, potentially highlighting Jesus as the new Moses bringing a new covenant. The book begins with a genealogy tracing Jesus' lineage from Abraham through David, establishing His credentials as the Messiah.

Throughout his account, Matthew emphasizes Jesus' role as the King of the Jews and the inaugurator of the Kingdom of Heaven. He frequently uses the phrase "to fulfill what was spoken through the prophet," underscoring how Jesus' life and ministry fulfill Old Testament prophecies. This approach serves to validate Jesus' messianic claims for a Jewish readership while also demonstrating the continuity between the Old and New Testaments.

Matthew's Gospel includes unique material not found in the other Gospels, such as the visit of the Magi, the flight to Egypt, and several parables. It also contains the most comprehensive account of Jesus' teachings, including the renowned Sermon on the Mount, which outlines the ethical and spiritual principles of the Kingdom of Heaven.

The narrative culminates in Jesus' crucifixion, resurrection, and the Great Commission, where He charges His disciples to make disciples of all nations. This ending emphasizes the universal scope of Jesus' mission and the call for His followers to continue His work.

KEY EVENTS, CHARACTERS, AND TEACHINGS:

- The genealogy and birth narrative of Jesus (Matt 1-2)

- John the Baptist's ministry and Jesus' baptism (Matt 3)

- The temptation in the wilderness (Matthew 4:1-11)

- The Sermon on the Mount (Matthew 5-7)

- Various miracles and healings performed by Jesus (throughout)

- The calling and commissioning of the twelve disciples (Matthew 10)

- Parables of the Kingdom (Matthew 13)

- The Transfiguration (Matthew 17:1-13)

- Jesus' triumphal entry into Jerusalem (Matthew 21:1-11)

- The Last Supper and Jesus' arrest (Matthew 26)

- The crucifixion and resurrection (Matthew 27-28)

- The Great Commission (Matthew 28:16-20)

EXPLORING SOME DEEPER MEANINGS:

1. The genealogy of Jesus (1:1-17) serves multiple purposes. It establishes Jesus' legal claim to the throne of David, demonstrates God's faithfulness across generations, and includes notable women and Gentiles, foreshadowing the inclusive nature of Jesus' mission.

2. The narrative of the Magi (2:1-12) introduces the theme of Gentile inclusion in God's plan and contrasts the recognition of Jesus by foreigners with the hostility of Israel's leaders.

3. The Sermon on the Mount (5-7) presents the ethical and spiritual core of Jesus' teaching. The Beatitudes (5:3-12) redefine blessing in God's kingdom, challenging conventional notions of success and happiness.

4. The Lord's Prayer (6:9-13) serves as a model for communication with God, emphasizing relationship, reverence, dependence, forgiveness, and spiritual protection.

5. The parables of the Kingdom (13) use everyday imagery to convey profound spiritual truths about the nature and growth of God's reign. They emphasize themes of hidden value, gradual growth, and final judgment.

6. Peter's confession of Jesus as the Messiah (16:13-20) marks a turning point in the Gospel. Jesus' response about building His church on this confession introduces ecclesiological themes that will be developed in later New Testament writings.

7. The Transfiguration (17:1-13) provides a glimpse of Jesus' divine glory and connects Him with the law (Moses) and the prophets (Elijah), affirming His supreme authority.

8. The cleansing of the Temple (21:12-17) symbolizes judgment on corrupt religious practices and the inauguration of a new form of worship centered on Jesus.

9. The Olivet Discourse (24-25) blends prophecies about the destruction of Jerusalem with teachings about the end times, challenging believers to live in constant readiness for Christ's return.

10. The institution of the Lord's Supper (26:26-29) reinterprets the Passover meal in light of Jesus' impending sacrifice, establishing a new covenant ritual for His followers.

11. The crucifixion narrative emphasizes Jesus' identity as the King of the Jews and includes unique elements like the earthquake and the raising of holy people (27:51-53), underscoring the cosmic significance of Jesus' death.

12. The Great Commission (28:16-20) expands the scope of Jesus' mission beyond Israel to all nations, emphasizing baptism, teaching, and the ongoing presence of Christ with His church.

Mark

BOOK SUMMARY:

The Gospel of Mark, traditionally attributed to John Mark, a companion of Peter and Paul, is widely considered to be the earliest written account of Jesus' life and ministry. Composed around 65-75 AD, Mark's Gospel is characterized by its fast-paced narrative style, vivid details, and emphasis on Jesus' actions rather than His extended teachings.

Mark presents Jesus as the suffering Servant-Messiah, focusing on His identity as the Son of God and His mission to serve and give His life as a ransom for many. The Gospel is structured around Jesus' journey from Galilee to Jerusalem, culminating in His crucifixion and resurrection. Mark's account is notable for its sense of urgency, frequently using the word "immediately" to transition between events.

The book begins abruptly with John the Baptist's ministry and Jesus' baptism, omitting any birth narrative. It then proceeds to recount Jesus' public ministry, including His teachings, healings, exorcisms, and conflicts with religious authorities. Mark pays particular attention to the disciples' struggles to understand Jesus' identity and mission, highlighting their confusion and failures alongside their moments of insight.

A key theme in Mark's Gospel is the "Messianic Secret," where Jesus often commands people to keep His identity and miracles secret. This theme underscores the paradoxical nature of Jesus' messiahship, which is fully revealed only through His suffering and death.

The narrative builds to a climax with Jesus' entry into Jerusalem, His final teachings, His last supper with the disciples, His arrest, trial, crucifixion, and resurrection. Mark's original ending at 16:8, with the women fleeing from the empty tomb in fear, leaves readers with a sense of awe and challenge, inviting them to consider their own response to the risen Christ.

KEY EVENTS, CHARACTERS, AND TEACHINGS:

- The ministry of John the Baptist and the baptism of Jesus, marking the beginning of Jesus' public ministry and His anointing by the Holy Spirit (Mark 1:1-11)

- The temptation of Jesus in the wilderness, demonstrating His victory over Satan and His preparation for ministry (Mark 1:12-13)

- The calling of the first disciples, highlighting the immediacy of their response to Jesus' invitation (Mark 1:16-20)

- The healing of the paralytic and the forgiveness of sins, illustrating Jesus' authority to forgive and His divine nature (Mark 2:1-12)

- The parables of the kingdom, revealing the mysteries of the kingdom of God through stories such as the Sower and the Seed (Mark 4:1-34)

- The calming of the storm and other miracles, emphasizing Jesus' authority over nature and His power to bring peace amidst chaos (Mark 4:35-41)

- The confession of Peter, acknowledging Jesus as the Christ, followed by Jesus' prediction of His suffering and resurrection (Mark 8:27-38)

- The Transfiguration, where Jesus' divine glory is revealed to Peter, James, and John, affirming His identity as the Son of God (Mark 9:2-13)

- The teachings on servanthood and greatness, exemplified by Jesus' life and mission (Mark 9:33-37, 10:42-45)

- The triumphal entry into Jerusalem, signifying Jesus' messianic kingship and the fulfillment of prophecy (Mark 11:1-11)

- The Passion narrative, detailing Jesus' arrest, trial, crucifixion, and the significance of His sacrificial death (Mark 14-15)

- The resurrection of Jesus, demonstrating His victory over sin and death, and the commissioning of the disciples to spread the Gospel (Mark 16)

EXPLORING SOME DEEPER MEANINGS:

1. The literary style of Mark is concise and action-oriented, with the frequent use of the word "immediately," creating a sense of urgency and movement in the narrative. This style reflects the dynamic nature of Jesus' ministry and the urgent call to respond to the Gospel.

2. The "Messianic Secret" is a recurring theme in Mark, where Jesus often instructs those He heals or who recognize His identity to keep silent. This motif highlights the unfolding revelation of Jesus' mission, emphasizing the need for the cross and the proper understanding of His messianic role.

3. The role of discipleship is central in Mark's Gospel, illustrating the challenges and costs associated with following Jesus. The disciples' misunderstandings and failures serve as a mirror for readers, inviting them to a deeper commitment and understanding of what it means to follow Christ.

4. The parables of the kingdom offer profound insights into the nature of God's kingdom, revealing truths about its growth, value, and accessibility. The parable of the Sower, for example, underscores the importance of receptive hearts in bearing spiritual fruit.

5. The miracle accounts in Mark not only demonstrate Jesus' divine authority but also serve as metaphors for spiritual truths. The calming of the storm, for instance, illustrates Jesus' power to bring peace amidst life's trials and challenges.

6. The Passion narrative is the culmination of Mark's Gospel, emphasizing the necessity of the cross and the sacrificial nature of Jesus' mission. It invites readers to reflect on the cost of discipleship and the call to take up one's cross and follow Him.

7. The resurrection account in Mark, though brief, is pivotal, affirming Jesus' victory over death and the hope of eternal life for believers. The empty tomb serves as a powerful testimony to the reality of the risen Christ and the promise of new beginnings.

8. The commissioning of the disciples at the end of Mark highlights the global scope of the Gospel message, urging believers to proclaim the good news to all creation. This call to mission underscores the transformative power of the Gospel and the responsibility of believers to share it with others.

9. The emphasis on servanthood is woven throughout Mark's Gospel, with Jesus modeling a life of humility, service, and sacrifice. His teachings on greatness and leadership challenge societal norms, inviting followers to embrace a countercultural way of living.

10. The interplay of faith and fear is a recurring theme, with Jesus often encouraging His followers to have faith in the face of fear and uncertainty. This dynamic is evident in the calming of the storm and the healing miracles, where faith is portrayed as the key to experiencing God's power and presence.

Luke
BOOK SUMMARY:

The Book of Luke, the third Gospel in the New Testament, is a detailed and orderly account of the life, ministry, death, and resurrection of Jesus Christ. Written by Luke, a physician and companion of the Apostle Paul, this Gospel emphasizes Jesus as the Savior of all people, highlighting His compassion for the marginalized and outcasts. Luke's narrative provides a comprehensive and chronological portrayal of Jesus' mission, showcasing His teachings, miracles, and the fulfillment of Old Testament prophecies.

Luke begins with the birth announcements of John the Baptist and Jesus, setting the stage for the arrival of the Messiah. The birth narrative of Jesus is rich with historical context and theological significance, emphasizing His humble beginnings and divine mission. As the narrative unfolds, Luke highlights Jesus' interactions with various individuals, demonstrating His love for sinners, the poor, women, and Gentiles.

Central to Luke's Gospel is the theme of salvation and the universal scope of God's redemptive plan. Jesus is portrayed as the compassionate Savior who brings hope and healing to all who are lost and broken. Through parables and teachings, Luke emphasizes the importance of repentance, faith, and the kingdom of God.

The Passion narrative in Luke underscores the fulfillment of prophecy and the necessity of Jesus' suffering and resurrection. Luke's account concludes with the ascension of Jesus and the commissioning of the disciples, preparing the way for the spread of the Gospel through the early church.

KEY EVENTS, CHARACTERS, AND TEACHINGS:

- The birth announcements and miraculous conceptions of John the Baptist and Jesus, highlighting God's intervention in history and the fulfillment of prophecy (Luke 1)

- The birth of Jesus, including the visit of the shepherds and the angelic proclamation of peace on earth (Luke 2:1-20)

- The presentation of Jesus at the temple and the prophetic declarations of Simeon and Anna (Luke 2:21-40)

- The ministry of John the Baptist, calling for repentance and preparing the way for Jesus (Luke 3:1-20)

- The genealogy of Jesus, tracing His lineage back to Adam, emphasizing His connection to all humanity (Luke 3:23-38)

- The temptation of Jesus, affirming His victory over Satan and His readiness for ministry (Luke 4:1-13)

- The sermon at Nazareth, where Jesus declares His mission to bring good news to the poor and oppressed (Luke 4:14-30)

- The calling of the first disciples and the miraculous catch of fish, illustrating the power of Jesus' word and the call to follow Him (Luke 5:1-11)

- The parables of mercy and forgiveness, such as the Good Samaritan and the Prodigal Son, revealing the heart of God toward sinners (Luke 10:25-37, 15:11-32)

- The teachings on prayer, including the Lord's Prayer and the parable of the persistent widow, emphasizing the importance of persistence and faith (Luke 11:1-13, 18:1-8)

- The account of Zacchaeus, a tax collector transformed by Jesus' love and grace (Luke 19:1-10)

- The triumphal entry into Jerusalem and Jesus' cleansing of the temple, signifying His messianic authority (Luke 19:28-48)

- The Passion narrative, detailing Jesus' arrest, trial, crucifixion, and the significance of His sacrificial death (Luke 22-23)

- The resurrection appearances and the road to Emmaus, affirming the reality of the risen Christ and the fulfillment of Scripture (Luke 24:1-35)

- The ascension of Jesus and the commissioning of the disciples, preparing them for the mission of spreading the Gospel (Luke 24:36-53)

EXPLORING SOME DEEPER MEANINGS:

1. The role of women in Luke is prominently featured, with stories of Mary, Elizabeth, Anna, and other women who play vital roles in the narrative. This emphasis highlights the inclusivity of Jesus' ministry and the dignity and value of women in God's kingdom.

2. The theme of joy and praise is woven throughout Luke's Gospel, with songs and hymns punctuating the narrative, such as Mary's Magnificat and the angels' proclamation at Jesus' birth. These expressions of joy reflect the hope and salvation brought by the Messiah.

3. The parables unique to Luke, such as the Good Samaritan and the Prodigal Son, convey profound truths about God's grace, mercy, and the call to love others.

These stories challenge cultural norms and invite readers to embody the compassion and forgiveness of Christ.

4. The emphasis on the Holy Spirit is notable in Luke, with frequent references to the Spirit's role in Jesus' ministry and the empowerment of His followers. This focus underscores the dependence on the Spirit for guidance and strength in fulfilling God's mission.

5. The connection between Jesus and the marginalized is a central theme, with Jesus often reaching out to the poor, sinners, and outcasts. This emphasis on social justice and compassion reflects the heart of God for all people, regardless of status or background.

6. The focus on prayer in Luke is evident in the frequent depiction of Jesus praying and His teachings on the importance of prayer. This theme highlights the necessity of communion with God and reliance on Him in all aspects of life and ministry.

7. The road to Emmaus story serves as a powerful illustration of Jesus' presence with His followers and the transformative power of recognizing Him in the breaking of bread. This narrative invites believers to encounter the risen Christ in everyday life and community.

8. The fulfillment of prophecy is a recurring theme in Luke, with numerous references to Old Testament prophecies and their realization in Jesus' life and mission. This emphasis reinforces the continuity of God's redemptive plan throughout Scripture.

9. The universal scope of salvation is highlighted in Luke, with the genealogy tracing Jesus' lineage to Adam and the message of salvation extending to all nations. This global perspective underscores the inclusivity of the Gospel and God's desire for all people to know Him.

10. The ascension of Jesus marks the transition from His earthly ministry to the mission of the early church, empowered by the Holy Spirit. This event underscores the ongoing work of Christ through His followers and the hope of His return.

John

BOOK SUMMARY:

The Book of John, the fourth Gospel in the New Testament, offers a unique and profound portrayal of Jesus Christ as the eternal Word and Son of God. Traditionally attributed to the Apostle John, this Gospel is distinct from the Synoptic Gospels (Matthew, Mark, and Luke) and focuses on the divine nature and mission of Jesus. Through a series of signs, teachings, and encounters, John presents Jesus as the source of life and light, emphasizing the themes of belief, love, and eternal life.

John begins with the majestic prologue that declares Jesus as the Word who was with God and is God, emphasizing His role in creation and His incarnation. The narrative then unfolds through a series of signs and miracles that reveal Jesus' identity and authority. Unlike the other Gospels, John places significant emphasis on Jesus' discourses and His interactions with individuals, such as Nicodemus and the Samaritan woman, offering deep theological insights into the nature of salvation and the kingdom of God.

The Gospel of John culminates in the Passion narrative, highlighting the fulfillment of Jesus' mission through His sacrificial death and victorious resurrection. John concludes with the post-resurrection appearances and the commissioning of the disciples, affirming the transformative power of the risen Christ and the call to share the Gospel.

KEY EVENTS, CHARACTERS, AND TEACHINGS:

- The prologue, which introduces Jesus as the Word and establishes His divine nature and role in creation (John 1:1-18)

- The testimony of John the Baptist, who identifies Jesus as the Lamb of God and the One who baptizes with the Holy Spirit (John 1:19-34)

- The calling of the first disciples, including Andrew, Peter, Philip, and Nathanael, highlighting their recognition of Jesus as the Messiah (John 1:35-51)

- The wedding at Cana, where Jesus performs His first miracle of turning water into wine, revealing His glory (John 2:1-11)

- The cleansing of the temple, demonstrating Jesus' authority and zeal for true worship (John 2:13-22)

- The conversation with Nicodemus, emphasizing the necessity of being born again and the promise of eternal life through belief in Jesus (John 3:1-21)

- The encounter with the Samaritan woman, illustrating Jesus' offer of living water and His inclusive mission (John 4:1-42)

- The healing at the pool of Bethesda, showcasing Jesus' compassion and authority over illness (John 5:1-15)

- The feeding of the five thousand and Jesus walking on water, emphasizing His provision and power over nature (John 6:1-21)

- The Bread of Life discourse, where Jesus declares Himself the true sustenance for eternal life (John 6:22-59)

- The healing of the man born blind, illustrating spiritual enlightenment and the transformative power of Jesus (John 9:1-41)

- The Good Shepherd discourse, highlighting Jesus' care for His followers and His sacrificial love (John 10:1-18)

- The raising of Lazarus, revealing Jesus as the resurrection and the life, and His power over death (John 11:1-44)

- The triumphal entry into Jerusalem, affirming Jesus as the King who comes in peace (John 12:12-19)

- The Last Supper and Jesus washing the disciples' feet, demonstrating servanthood and love (John 13:1-17)

- The Farewell Discourses, where Jesus comforts His disciples and promises the Holy Spirit (John 14-16)

- The High Priestly Prayer, expressing Jesus' desire for unity and glory for His followers (John 17)

- The Passion narrative, detailing Jesus' arrest, trial, crucifixion, and His fulfillment of Scripture (John 18-19)

- The resurrection appearances, including Jesus' interactions with Mary Magdalene, Thomas, and the disciples, affirming His victory over death (John 20:1-29)

- The reinstatement of Peter, highlighting forgiveness and the call to shepherd God's people (John 21:15-19)

EXPLORING SOME DEEPER MEANINGS:

1. The concept of the Word (Logos) is central to John's theology, presenting Jesus as the divine Logos who became flesh, bridging the gap between God and humanity. This foundational theme emphasizes the incarnation and Jesus' role in revealing God's character.

2. The "I AM" statements in John, such as "I am the Bread of Life" and "I am the Light of the World," affirm Jesus' divine identity and His fulfillment of Old Testament themes, inviting readers to explore the depth of His nature and mission.

3. The symbolism of light and darkness is prevalent throughout John, illustrating the contrast between belief and unbelief, spiritual enlightenment and blindness, and the transformative power of encountering Christ.

4. The theme of belief is woven throughout the Gospel, with John emphasizing the importance of faith in Jesus as the means to eternal life. This theme challenges readers to respond personally to Jesus' invitation and to trust in His redemptive work.

5. The role of the Holy Spirit is highlighted in John's Gospel, with Jesus promising the Spirit as the Comforter, Advocate, and source of truth for His followers. This focus underscores the Spirit's role in guiding, empowering, and sustaining believers.

6. The intimate portrayal of Jesus' relationships, especially with His disciples, provides a rich exploration of love, friendship, and the call to follow Him. John's Gospel invites readers into a deeper understanding of Jesus' relational nature and His desire for communion with His people.

7. The focus on signs and miracles in John serves to reveal Jesus' divine authority and to invite belief in Him. Each sign points to a deeper spiritual truth, encouraging readers to seek understanding beyond the miraculous.

8. The duality of love and sacrifice is central to John's narrative, exemplified in Jesus' teachings and actions, culminating in His ultimate sacrifice on the cross. This theme calls believers to emulate Christ's selfless love in their own lives.

9. The exploration of truth and testimony is significant in John, with Jesus presenting Himself as the embodiment of truth and His works and words serving as a witness to His identity and mission.

10. The restoration and commissioning of Peter in the final chapter underscores themes of forgiveness, redemption, and purpose, highlighting the transformative impact of the risen Christ on His followers and the ongoing mission of the church.

Acts

BOOK SUMMARY:

The Book of Acts, also known as the Acts of the Apostles, serves as a continuation of the Gospel of Luke, chronicling the spread of the early church and the work of the Holy Spirit. Authored by Luke, Acts provides a historical account of the church's growth from Jerusalem to the ends of the earth, highlighting the transformative power of the Gospel and the role of the apostles in fulfilling the Great Commission. This book emphasizes the transition from Jesus' earthly ministry to the empowerment and mission of His followers, showcasing the dynamic spread of Christianity in the first century.

Acts begins with the ascension of Jesus and the outpouring of the Holy Spirit at Pentecost, marking the birth of the church. The narrative follows the apostles, particularly Peter and Paul, as they preach the Gospel, perform miracles, and establish communities of believers across diverse regions. Acts illustrates the church's expansion, overcoming persecution, and addressing challenges such as cultural diversity and theological disputes.

Central to the book is the theme of the Holy Spirit's guidance and empowerment, enabling ordinary believers to accomplish extraordinary feats in spreading the Gospel. Acts highlights the importance of prayer, fellowship, and bold proclamation, showcasing the church's unity and dedication to Christ's mission.

KEY EVENTS, CHARACTERS, AND TEACHINGS:

- The ascension of Jesus and the promise of the Holy Spirit, preparing the apostles for their mission (Acts 1:1-11

- The selection of Matthias as a replacement for Judas, demonstrating the importance of leadership and apostolic succession (Acts 1:12-26)

- The coming of the Holy Spirit at Pentecost, empowering the apostles and resulting in the conversion of thousands (Acts 2:1-41)

- The early church community, characterized by devotion to teaching, fellowship, breaking of bread, and prayer (Acts 2:42-47)

- The healing of the lame man at the temple, illustrating the apostles' authority and the power of Jesus' name (Acts 3:1-10)

- The arrest and trial of Peter and John, showcasing their boldness in proclaiming the Gospel despite persecution (Acts 4:1-22)

- The account of Ananias and Sapphira, emphasizing the seriousness of integrity and honesty within the church (Acts 5:1-11)

- The selection of the seven deacons, including Stephen and Philip, to address the needs of the growing community (Acts 6:1-7)

- The martyrdom of Stephen, the first Christian martyr, whose testimony and vision of Jesus highlight the cost of discipleship (Acts 6:8-7:60)

- The conversion of Saul (Paul) on the road to Damascus, a pivotal moment marking the transformation of a persecutor into a key apostle (Acts 9:1-19)

- The ministry of Peter, including the healing of Aeneas and the raising of Tabitha, demonstrating God's power through the apostles (Acts 9:32-43)

- The vision of Peter and the conversion of Cornelius, a Gentile, signifying the opening of the Gospel to all nations (Acts 10)

- The council at Jerusalem, addressing the inclusion of Gentiles and affirming salvation by grace through faith (Acts 15:1-29)

- Paul's missionary journeys, establishing churches and spreading the Gospel across Asia Minor and Europe (Acts 13-21)

- Paul's arrest and trials, highlighting his unwavering commitment to the Gospel and defense of the faith (Acts 21-26)

- Paul's journey to Rome, demonstrating God's providence and the fulfillment of the Gospel reaching the heart of the Roman Empire (Acts 27-28)

EXPLORING SOME DEEPER MEANINGS:

1. The role of the Holy Spirit is central to Acts, empowering the apostles and guiding the early church in its mission. The Spirit's presence and power are evident in miraculous events, bold proclamations, and the unity of believers.

2. The theme of witness and mission is prominent, as the apostles fulfill Jesus' command to be His witnesses "in Jerusalem, and in all Judea and Samaria, and to the ends of the earth" (Acts 1:8). This theme underscores the church's global mission and the spread of the Gospel.

3. The importance of community is highlighted in the early church's practices of fellowship, sharing resources, and mutual support. These communal aspects reflect the unity and love that characterize the body of Christ.

4. The expansion of the church despite persecution illustrates God's sovereignty and the unstoppable nature of His plan. Acts demonstrates how opposition often leads to greater opportunities for the Gospel to spread.

5. The inclusion of Gentiles marks a significant turning point in the church's history, as the Gospel transcends cultural and ethnic barriers. This inclusivity reflects the universal scope of God's salvation.

6. The transformation of individuals, such as Saul's conversion to Paul, highlights the power of the Gospel to change lives and redirect destinies. Acts emphasizes the transformative work of Christ in individuals and communities.

7. The importance of leadership is evident in the selection of apostles, deacons, and elders to guide and serve the church. Acts underscores the need for wise and Spirit-led leadership in advancing God's kingdom.

8. Theological and cultural challenges faced by the early church, such as the debate over circumcision, illustrate the need for discernment and unity in addressing complex issues. The Jerusalem Council serves as a model for resolving disputes with grace and truth.

9. The commitment to prayer and worship is evident throughout Acts, as the early believers seek God's guidance and strength in all aspects of their mission. This emphasis on prayer reflects the dependence of the church on divine power and direction.

10. The narrative of Paul's journeys highlights God's providence and protection in fulfilling His purposes. Despite trials and hardships, Paul's unwavering dedication to the Gospel serves as an inspiration for all believers.

Romans
BOOK SUMMARY:

The Book of Romans, authored by the Apostle Paul, is a profound theological treatise that systematically presents the doctrine of salvation through faith in Jesus Christ. Written to the Christian community in Rome, this epistle addresses both Jewish and Gentile believers, providing a comprehensive explanation of the Gospel's power to reconcile humanity with God. Romans is foundational for understanding Christian theology, emphasizing themes of grace, righteousness, and the transformative power of the Spirit.

Romans begins by highlighting humanity's universal need for salvation due to sin, establishing the inability of the Law to achieve righteousness. Paul then explains how righteousness is obtained through faith in Christ, who provides justification and peace with God. The epistle explores the believer's new life in the Spirit, the implications of God's sovereign election, and the ethical responsibilities of living as part of the body of Christ.

Central to Romans is the concept of justification by faith, which frees believers from the condemnation of the Law and empowers them to live in the Spirit's transformative power. Paul also addresses practical issues within the church, promoting unity and love among believers of diverse backgrounds.

KEY THEMES, CONCEPTS, AND TEACHINGS:

- The power of the Gospel as the means of salvation for everyone who believes, revealing God's righteousness (Romans 1:16-17)

- Humanity's universal sinfulness and the consequences of rejecting God, highlighting the need for divine intervention (Romans 1:18-32)

- The inadequacy of the Law to achieve righteousness, demonstrating the necessity of faith in Christ (Romans 2-3

- Justification by faith, as exemplified by Abraham, and the imputation of righteousness apart from works (Romans 4)

- The benefits of justification, including peace with God, access to grace, and the hope of glory (Romans 5:1-11)

- The contrast between Adam and Christ, illustrating the reign of sin versus the reign of grace (Romans 5:12-21)

- The believer's union with Christ, leading to freedom from sin and the call to live a new life in the Spirit (Romans 6)

- The struggle between the flesh and the Spirit, highlighting the believer's ongoing battle with sin and the Spirit's victory (Romans 7-8)

- God's sovereign election and faithfulness to Israel, affirming His promises and plan for both Jews and Gentiles (Romans 9-11)

- The practical implications of the Gospel, including living as a living sacrifice, using spiritual gifts, and pursuing love and unity (Romans 12-13)

- The call for mutual acceptance and understanding between Jewish and Gentile believers, emphasizing love and liberty (Romans 14-15)

EXPLORING SOME DEEPER MEANINGS:

1. The theme of justification by faith is central to Romans, emphasizing that righteousness comes through faith in Jesus Christ, not through adherence to the Law. This concept underscores the transformative power of grace and the believer's new standing before God.

2. The universality of sin is a foundational theme, highlighting the shared human condition of sinfulness and the resulting separation from God. Romans underscores the need for a Savior and the impossibility of achieving righteousness through human effort.

3. The contrast between Adam and Christ illustrates the theological concept of original sin and the redemptive work of Christ as the new Adam, whose obedience and sacrifice bring life and reconciliation.

4. The role of the Holy Spirit in the believer's life is emphasized in Romans 8, highlighting the Spirit's work in empowering believers to live according to God's will, assuring them of their identity as God's children, and interceding on their behalf.

5. The sovereignty of God in election and His faithfulness to His promises are explored in Romans 9-11. Paul addresses the tension between God's sovereignty and human responsibility, affirming that God's purposes will ultimately prevail.

6. The transformation of the believer's life is a key theme, as Paul calls Christians to present themselves as living sacrifices and to be transformed by the renewing of their minds. This transformation results in practical expressions of love, service, and humility.

7. The importance of unity and love within the diverse body of Christ is emphasized, as Paul urges believers to accept one another and to prioritize love over personal convictions. This call to unity reflects the Gospel's power to reconcile and unite people of different backgrounds.

8. The concept of Christian liberty is addressed, encouraging believers to consider the conscience and convictions of others while exercising their freedom in Christ. Paul emphasizes that love should guide behavior, particularly in matters of disputable issues.

9. The relationship between law and grace is a recurring theme, as Paul explains that the Law reveals sin but cannot save. Grace, on the other hand, provides the means for salvation and empowers believers to live in obedience to God.

10. The missional aspect of the Gospel is highlighted as Paul expresses his desire to visit Rome and share the Gospel with both Jews and Gentiles. This missional focus underscores the global nature of the Gospel and the call to proclaim it to all nations.

1 Corinthians

BOOK SUMMARY:

The Book of 1 Corinthians, authored by the Apostle Paul, addresses the challenges and issues faced by the early Christian community in Corinth. This epistle offers practical guidance and theological insights to help the church navigate divisions, moral issues, and questions about Christian living. Paul's letter emphasizes the importance of unity, love, and holiness, urging the Corinthians to live in a manner that reflects their identity in Christ.

Written to a diverse and cosmopolitan congregation, 1 Corinthians tackles a wide range of topics, including divisions within the church, sexual immorality, disputes among believers, and questions about marriage, spiritual gifts, and the resurrection. Paul provides corrective teachings and encourages the Corinthians to embrace the wisdom and power of the Gospel in every aspect of their lives.

Central to 1 Corinthians is the theme of unity in the body of Christ, which Paul emphasizes through the analogy of the church as a single body with many members. The letter also highlights the supremacy of love as the guiding principle for all Christian conduct.

KEY THEMES, ISSUES, AND TEACHINGS:

- Divisions within the church, calling for unity and humility, emphasizing that Christ is the foundation of their faith (1 Corinthians 1-4)

- Addressing sexual immorality, calling for purity and discipline within the community (1 Corinthians 5-6)

- Guidance on marriage and singleness, offering practical advice on relationships and the sanctity of marriage (1 Corinthians 7)

- Disputes among believers, encouraging resolution within the church and highlighting the importance of living out Christian values (1 Corinthians 6)

- Food offered to idols, addressing issues of conscience and the importance of love over knowledge (1 Corinthians 8-10)

- The proper conduct of worship, including teachings on head coverings and the Lord's Supper (1 Corinthians 11)

- The use of spiritual gifts, emphasizing their purpose for building up the church and the necessity of love as the greatest gift (1 Corinthians 12-14)

- The resurrection of Christ, affirming the foundational importance of the resurrection and its implications for believers (1 Corinthians 15)

- The collection for the saints, demonstrating the importance of generosity and support for the broader Christian community (1 Corinthians 16)

EXPLORING SOME DEEPER MEANINGS:

1. The theme of unity and diversity is central to 1 Corinthians, particularly in Paul's analogy of the church as a body with many parts. He emphasizes that every member is essential and that unity is found in diversity when each part contributes to the whole.

2. The supremacy of love, especially in 1 Corinthians 13, underscores the importance of love as the guiding principle for all Christian behavior. Paul describes love as patient, kind, and enduring, highlighting its eternal nature and centrality in the Christian life.

3. The resurrection of Christ is a cornerstone of Christian faith, as detailed in 1 Corinthians **15.** Paul affirms the historical reality of the resurrection and its significance as the guarantee of believers' future resurrection and eternal life.

4. The role of spiritual gifts is to edify the church, and Paul encourages their use with love and order. He distinguishes between gifts and stresses that all gifts are valuable and should be used for the common good.

5. The call to holiness and purity is evident in Paul's instructions regarding sexual immorality and the importance of honoring God with one's body. He urges believers to flee from immorality and to glorify God in their conduct.

6. The importance of resolving disputes internally reflects the call for believers to live out their faith in practical ways, demonstrating wisdom and maturity in handling conflicts and disagreements.

7. The tension between knowledge and love is addressed in the discussion of food offered to idols. Paul emphasizes that while knowledge can lead to pride, love builds up and prioritizes the well-being of others.

8. The sanctity of marriage and singleness is affirmed, with Paul providing guidance on relationships, highlighting the value of both states and encouraging believers to live according to their calling.

9. The proper conduct of worship involves maintaining order and honoring traditions while focusing on the edification and unity of the church. Paul addresses issues of decorum and the significance of the Lord's Supper as a communal act of remembrance and proclamation of the Lord's death.

10. The theme of generosity and support for the broader Christian community is reflected in Paul's instructions about the collection for the saints in Jerusalem, encouraging believers to give generously and willingly.

2 Corinthians
BOOK SUMMARY:

The Book of 2 Corinthians, authored by the Apostle Paul, is a deeply personal and heartfelt letter that addresses the challenges and struggles faced by the apostle in his relationship with the Corinthian church. This epistle reflects Paul's defense of his apostleship, his profound concern for the spiritual welfare of the Corinthians, and his joy in their repentance and growth in faith. Through 2 Corinthians, Paul provides insights into the nature of Christian ministry, the reality of suffering, and the transformative power of God's grace.

Written in the aftermath of a painful visit and a sorrowful letter, 2 Corinthians expresses Paul's relief and gratitude upon hearing of the Corinthians' positive response. The letter is a rich tapestry of personal reflections, theological teachings, and practical guidance, aimed at strengthening the church and affirming Paul's role as a true apostle of Christ.

Central to 2 Corinthians is the theme of strength through weakness, as Paul shares his own experiences of suffering and divine comfort, highlighting the paradox of finding strength in vulnerability and grace in adversity.

KEY THEMES, ISSUES, AND TEACHINGS:

- Paul's defense of his apostleship, addressing accusations and affirming his calling and integrity (2 Corinthians 1-7)

- The comfort and encouragement in suffering, emphasizing God's compassion and the purpose of trials (2 Corinthians 1:3-11)

- The ministry of reconciliation, highlighting the role of believers as ambassadors for Christ (2 Corinthians 5:11-21)

- The collection for the saints in Jerusalem, encouraging generosity and the principles of Christian giving (2 Corinthians 8-9)

- Paul's personal reflections on weakness and strength, illustrating the sufficiency of God's grace (2 Corinthians 10-13)

- The nature of Christian ministry, characterized by sincerity, humility, and reliance on God's power (2 Corinthians 4:1-18)

- Paul's visions and revelations, including his experience of being caught up to the third heaven (2 Corinthians 12:1-10)

EXPLORING SOME DEEPER MEANINGS:

1. The theme of strength in weakness is central to 2 Corinthians, as Paul reveals his own struggles and the sufficiency of God's grace. He emphasizes that God's power is made perfect in human weakness.

2. The ministry of reconciliation underscores the believer's role as an ambassador for Christ, tasked with proclaiming the message of reconciliation between God and humanity.

3. The comfort in suffering reflects Paul's personal experience of divine consolation amid trials, offering encouragement to believers facing their own hardships. Paul teaches that suffering can lead to greater reliance on God and empathy for others.

4. The principles of Christian giving are articulated in Paul's exhortation to contribute to the collection for the Jerusalem church. He emphasizes cheerful and sacrificial giving, grounded in the example of Christ's generosity.

5. The nature of authentic Christian ministry is described in terms of sincerity, humility, and reliance on God's power rather than human credentials. Paul contrasts his own approach with that of false apostles, highlighting the importance of integrity and faithfulness.

6. Paul's defense of his apostleship is woven throughout the letter, as he addresses accusations and affirms his commitment to the Gospel. He defends his authority and character, emphasizing the legitimacy of his ministry.

7. The reality of spiritual warfare is acknowledged as Paul describes the challenges he faces in his ministry. He encourages believers to be vigilant and to rely on God's strength to overcome opposition and spiritual struggles.

8. The transformative power of grace is a recurring theme, as Paul testifies to the impact of God's grace in his own life and ministry. He highlights grace as the means of overcoming sin, weakness, and adversity.

9. Paul's visions and revelations offer a glimpse into his unique relationship with God and his understanding of spiritual realities. His experience of being caught up to the third heaven illustrates the profound encounters that shaped his ministry.

10. The call to holiness and repentance is emphasized as Paul encourages the Corinthians to examine themselves and pursue purity in their walk with Christ. He urges them to live in a manner worthy of their calling, reflecting the holiness of God.

Galatians

The Book of Galatians, authored by the Apostle Paul, is a passionate and urgent letter that addresses the issue of legalism and the defense of the Gospel of grace. Written to the churches in the region of Galatia, this epistle confronts the false teaching that Gentile believers must adhere to Jewish law, specifically circumcision, to be saved. Paul emphatically asserts that salvation is by grace through faith in Christ alone, apart from the works of the Law.

Galatians is a foundational text for understanding the doctrine of justification by faith and the believer's freedom in Christ. Paul's letter is both a theological treatise and a personal appeal, urging the Galatians to reject false teachings and to stand firm in the freedom that Christ has provided.

Central to Galatians is the contrast between law and grace, bondage and freedom, flesh and Spirit. Paul emphasizes that the true Gospel liberates believers from the bondage of legalism and empowers them to live by the Spirit.

KEY THEMES, ISSUES, AND TEACHINGS:

- Paul's defense of his apostolic authority, affirming the divine origin of his Gospel and his mission to the Gentiles (Galatians 1-2)

- Justification by faith, establishing that believers are made right with God through faith in Christ, not by works of the Law (Galatians 2:15-21)

- The role of the Law, explaining its purpose as a guardian until the coming of Christ and its inability to bring about salvation (Galatians 3:1-25)

- The believer's identity in Christ, highlighting the equality and unity of all believers as children of God through faith (Galatians 3:26-4:7)

- Freedom in Christ, urging believers to stand firm against legalism and to live in the freedom of the Gospel (Galatians 5:1-15)

- Life in the Spirit, contrasting the works of the flesh with the fruit of the Spirit and encouraging a Spirit-led life (Galatians 5:16-26)

- The law of Christ, emphasizing the call to bear one another's burdens and to live out the love and grace of Christ (Galatians 6:1-10)

EXPLORING SOME DEEPER MEANINGS:

1. The theme of justification by faith is central to Galatians, as Paul argues that righteousness comes through faith in Jesus Christ alone, not through adherence to the Law. This principle underscores the sufficiency of Christ's sacrifice and the believer's reliance on grace.

2. The purpose of the Law is addressed as Paul explains that the Law was given as a temporary guardian to lead people to Christ. The Law reveals sin but cannot save, highlighting the need for a Savior and the fulfillment of the Law in Christ.

3. The believer's freedom in Christ is a key theme, as Paul urges the Galatians to reject legalism and to embrace the liberty provided by the Gospel. This freedom is not a license to sin but an empowerment to live a life pleasing to God.

4. The contrast between flesh and Spirit is explored in Paul's teachings on the Christian life. He encourages believers to walk by the Spirit, producing the fruit of love, joy, peace, and other virtues that reflect the character of Christ.

5. The unity and equality of believers is emphasized as Paul declares that in Christ, there is neither Jew nor Gentile, slave nor free, male nor female. This radical equality underscores the inclusivity of the Gospel and the oneness of the body of Christ.

6. Paul's defense of his apostolic authority is woven throughout the letter, as he refutes accusations and asserts the divine origin of his message. He emphasizes that his Gospel came directly from Christ and is not subject to human authority.

7. The law of Christ, described as bearing one another's burdens, highlights the ethical implications of the Gospel. Paul calls believers to live out their faith through acts of love, service, and mutual support.

8. The danger of legalism is a recurring theme, as Paul warns against adding human requirements to the Gospel. He stresses that any attempt to earn salvation through works undermines the grace of God and nullifies the work of Christ.

9. The promise to Abraham is fulfilled in Christ, as Paul explains that those who have faith are children of Abraham and heirs according to the promise. This highlights the continuity of God's plan and the inclusion of Gentiles in the covenant.

10. The call to perseverance and faithfulness is evident as Paul encourages the Galatians to remain steadfast in their faith and to not grow weary in doing good. He assures them that they will reap a harvest if they do not give up.

Ephesians

BOOK SUMMARY:

The Epistle to the Ephesians is a profound and rich letter written by the Apostle Paul, unveiling the glorious mystery of the Church as the body of Christ. Composed while Paul was imprisoned in Rome, this epistle highlights the spiritual blessings and privileges of being united with Christ and encourages believers to live lives worthy of their divine calling.

Ephesians opens with a powerful theological section, expounding on the eternal plan of God to redeem and unite all things in Christ. Paul emphasizes the believers' position in Christ, their election, adoption, and redemption through His grace. He then shifts his focus to the practical implications of this glorious reality, exhorting believers to walk in unity, purity, and spiritual wisdom.

Central to the letter is the magnificent truth of the Church as the body of Christ, composed of both Jews and Gentiles, united by the transforming power of the gospel. Paul underscores the necessity of maintaining the unity of the Spirit through the bond of peace, while also addressing the diversity of gifts and roles within the Church.

Throughout the epistle, Paul emphasizes the believer's spiritual warfare against the forces of darkness and the importance of putting on the full armor of God. He concludes with a call to steadfastness, prayer, and the proclamation of the gospel, reminding believers of their identity as ambassadors of Christ.

<u>KEY EVENTS, CHARACTERS, AND TEACHINGS:</u>

- The spiritual blessings in Christ and the plan of redemption (Ephesians 1-2)

- The revelation of the mystery of the Church as the body of Christ (Ephesians 3)

- The call to walk in unity, maintaining the bond of peace (Ephesians 4:1-6)

- The diversity of gifts and roles within the Church (Ephesians 4:7-16)

- The exhortation to walk in purity, putting off the old self and being renewed in Christ (Ephesians 4:17-32)

- Instructions for holy living and godly relationships (Ephesians 5:1-21)

- Principles for marriage, family, and work relationships (Ephesians 5:22-6:9)

- The call to stand firm in spiritual warfare and put on the full armor of God (Ephesians 6:10-20)

- The role of the Apostle Paul as a minister and ambassador of the gospel (Ephesians 3:1-13, 6:19-20)

- The closing benediction and blessings (Ephesians 6:21-24

<u>EXPLORING SOME DEEPER MEANINGS:</u>

1. The doctrine of predestination and election (Ephesians 1:4-6) underscores God's sovereign choice and gracious plan of redemption, while emphasizing the believer's security and assurance in Christ.

2. The imagery of the Church as the "body of Christ" (Ephesians 1:22-23, 4:15-16) highlights the organic unity and interdependence of believers, with Christ as the head and source of life and growth.

3. The concept of being "seated with Christ in the heavenly realms" (Ephesians 2:6) represents the believer's spiritual position and authority in Christ, foreshadowing the ultimate inheritance and reign with Him.

4. The "mystery of Christ" (Ephesians 3:4-6) refers to the inclusion of the Gentiles in God's redemptive plan, breaking down the dividing wall of hostility and creating a new, unified humanity in Christ.

5. The "one new man" (Ephesians 2:15) symbolizes the reconciliation of Jews and Gentiles in the Church, transcending ethnic and cultural divisions through the peace accomplished by Christ's sacrifice.

6. The call to "walk worthy of the calling" (Ephesians 4:1) emphasizes the believer's responsibility to live a life that reflects the values and virtues of the gospel, manifesting the fruit of the Spirit.

7. The teachings on spiritual gifts and roles (Ephesians 4:7-16) highlight the diversity within the body of Christ and the importance of using one's gifts to build up the Church and foster unity and maturity.

8. The contrast between the "old self" and the "new self" (Ephesians 4:17-24) underscores the transformative power of the gospel and the call to daily renewal and personal holiness.

9. The teachings on relationships (Ephesians 5:22-6:9) elevate the principles of mutual submission, love, and respect, reflecting the profound love between Christ and the Church.

10. The metaphor of the "full armor of God" (Ephesians 6:10-20) equips believers for spiritual warfare against the schemes of the devil, underscoring the need for spiritual preparedness and reliance on God's strength.

11. The concept of being "ambassadors for Christ" (Ephesians 6:20) highlights the believer's role as representatives and ministers of reconciliation, proclaiming the gospel of peace to a world in need of redemption.

12. The recurring emphasis on the "mystery" (Ephesians 1:9, 3:3-6, 5:32) underscores the profound and once-hidden truths now revealed through Christ, inviting believers to continually explore and appreciate the depths of God's wisdom and grace.

Philippians

The Epistle to the Philippians, written by the Apostle Paul during his imprisonment in Rome, is a letter overflowing with joy, encouragement, and gratitude. Addressed to the believers in the city of Philippi, this epistle stands as a testament to the transformative power of the gospel and the importance of maintaining unity, humility, and steadfastness in the face of adversity.

In this letter, Paul expresses his deep affection for the Philippian church, commending them for their partnership in the gospel and their unwavering support during his imprisonment. He encourages them to remain united in love and purpose, exhorting them to have the same mindset as Christ, who humbled Himself and became obedient unto death on the cross.

A central theme of Philippians is the call to rejoice in all circumstances, as Paul exemplifies a life marked by contentment and trust in God's sovereign plan. He challenges the believers to press on toward the goal of knowing Christ more fully, pursuing spiritual maturity and living as citizens of heaven while navigating the challenges of life on earth.

Throughout the epistle, Paul emphasizes the importance of standing firm in the face of opposition, holding fast to the truth of the gospel, and maintaining a Christ-like attitude of selflessness, humility, and sacrificial love.

<u>KEY EVENTS, CHARACTERS, AND TEACHINGS:</u>

- Paul's expression of affection and gratitude for the Philippian church (Philippians 1:3-11)

- Paul's testimony of the advancement of the gospel despite his imprisonment (Philippians 1:12-26)

- The exhortation to stand firm in unity and steadfastness (Philippians 1:27-30)

- The call to have the mind of Christ, who humbled Himself and became obedient unto death (Philippians 2:1-11)

- The encouragement to work out personal salvation with fear and trembling (Philippians 2:12-18)

- The example of Timothy and Epaphroditus as faithful servants of Christ (Philippians 2:19-30)

- The warning against false teachers and the call to pursue the knowledge of Christ (Philippians 3:1-16)

- The citizenship of believers in heaven and the transformation of their bodies (Philippians 3:17-21)

- The exhortation to rejoice in the Lord always and to maintain a spirit of peace and contentment (Philippians 4:4-13)

- Paul's gratitude for the Philippians' financial support and the provision of God (Philippians 4:14-23)

EXPLORING SOME DEEPER MEANINGS:

1. The concept of "rejoicing in the Lord" (Philippians 4:4) highlights the source of true joy, which transcends external circumstances and is rooted in the believer's relationship with Christ.

2. The call to have the "mind of Christ" (Philippians 2:5-11) underscores the importance of humility, selflessness, and obedience, reflecting the profound example set by Christ in His incarnation, sacrificial death, and exaltation.

3. The imagery of "pressing on toward the goal" (Philippians 3:12-14) represents the believer's pursuit of spiritual maturity and the ultimate prize of knowing Christ more intimately, reflecting the ongoing process of sanctification.

4. The concept of being "citizens of heaven" (Philippians 3:20) reminds believers of their true identity and allegiance, living as ambassadors of Christ's kingdom while awaiting the transformation of their bodies and the fullness of their salvation.

5. The importance of unity and like-mindedness (Philippians 2:2-4) emphasizes the necessity of preserving the bond of love and harmony within the body of Christ, putting aside selfish ambition and vain conceit.

6. The example of Timothy and Epaphroditus (Philippians 2:19-30) highlights the qualities of faithful servants of Christ, characterized by selfless concern for others, diligence, and a willingness to sacrifice for the sake of the gospel.

7. The warning against false teachers and the call to pursue the knowledge of Christ (Philippians 3:1-11) underscores the importance of discernment, rejecting legalism and self-righteousness, and embracing the surpassing worth of knowing Christ and attaining the righteousness that comes through faith.

8. The concept of "working out personal salvation" (Philippians 2:12-13) emphasizes the believer's responsibility to actively participate in the process of sanctification, while acknowledging the empowering work of the Holy Spirit in their lives.

9. The principle of contentment and peace (Philippians 4:6-7, 11-13) highlights the believer's ability to find satisfaction and tranquility in any circumstance, trusting in God's provision and strength.

10. The model of partnership and support (Philippians 1:3-5, 4:14-19) reflects the importance of mutual encouragement, prayer, and practical assistance within the body of Christ, fostering a spirit of unity and care for one another's needs.

Colossians
BOOK SUMMARY:

The Epistle to the Colossians, authored by the Apostle Paul, is a profound letter that exalts the supremacy and preeminence of Jesus Christ. Written from prison, this epistle addresses the dangers of false teachings that were threatening to undermine the faith of the believers in Colossae.

Paul begins by affirming the truth of the gospel and the believers' faith in Christ. He then launches into a magnificent Christological passage, proclaiming the deity and supremacy of Christ as the image of the invisible God and the creator of all things. Paul emphasizes that in Christ, the fullness of deity dwells, and through Him, believers are reconciled to God.

Central to the letter is the warning against false philosophies and human traditions that devalue the sufficiency of Christ. Paul urges the Colossians to remain firmly rooted in Christ, rejecting religious legalism and ascetic practices that promote self-made religion rather than genuine spiritual growth.

The epistle also addresses practical matters of Christian living, encouraging believers to put off the old self and put on the new self, which is being renewed in the image of the Creator. Paul provides instructions for various relationships, including marriage, family, and work, emphasizing the principles of mutual submission, love, and respect.

Throughout the letter, Paul emphasizes the supremacy of Christ and the completeness of the believer's identity and spiritual resources in Him. The epistle concludes with exhortations to steadfastness, prayer, and wise conduct towards outsiders, reflecting the believer's role as a witness for Christ.

KEY EVENTS, CHARACTERS, AND TEACHINGS:

- The truth of the gospel and the believers' faith in Christ (Colossians 1:1-8)

- The supremacy and preeminence of Christ as the image of the invisible God (Colossians 1:15-20)

- The reconciliation of believers to God through Christ's sacrificial death (Colossians 1:21-23)

- Paul's ministry and suffering for the sake of the Church (Colossians 1:24-2:5)

- The warning against false philosophies and human traditions (Colossians 2:6-23)

- The call to put off the old self and put on the new self in Christ (Colossians 3:1-17)

- Instructions for Christian households and relationships (Colossians 3:18-4:1)

- The exhortation to steadfastness, prayer, and wise conduct (Colossians 4:2-6)

- Personal greetings and final instructions (Colossians 4:7-18)

EXPLORING SOME DEEPER MEANINGS:

1. The Christological hymn (Colossians 1:15-20) reveals the preeminence of Christ as the image of the invisible God, the firstborn over all creation, and the head of the Church. It affirms Christ's role in creation, redemption, and the reconciliation of all things to God.

2. The concept of the "fullness of deity" dwelling in Christ (Colossians 1:19, 2:9) emphasizes the complete and absolute sufficiency of Christ, refuting any need for additional philosophies or religious practices.

3. The imagery of being "rooted and built up in Christ" (Colossians 2:7) represents the believer's firm foundation in Christ and the importance of growing deeper in their relationship with Him.

4. The warning against "philosophy and empty deceit" (Colossians 2:8) underscores the danger of human traditions and false teachings that undermine the truth of the gospel and the supremacy of Christ.

5. The contrast between "self-made religion" and genuine spiritual growth (Colossians 2:16-23) highlights the futility of legalistic practices and the importance of seeking true spiritual nourishment in Christ.

6. The putting off of the "old self" and putting on the "new self" (Colossians 3:5-17) represents the believer's transformation through the renewal of their mind and the process of sanctification in Christ.

7. The teachings on Christian households and relationships (Colossians 3:18-4:1) emphasize the principles of mutual submission, love, and respect, reflecting the believer's new identity in Christ.

8. The call to steadfastness (Colossians 1:23, 4:2)
underscores the importance of perseverance and
unwavering commitment to the faith, even in the face of
challenges or persecution.

9. The emphasis on prayer (Colossians 4:2-4) highlights
the vital role of communication with God and the need for
believers to be watchful and thankful in their prayer lives.

10. The exhortation to wise conduct towards outsiders
(Colossians 4:5-6) reflects the believer's role as a witness
for Christ, engaging the world with grace, wisdom, and the
message of the gospel.

1 Thessalonians

BOOK SUMMARY:

The First Epistle to the Thessalonians, written by the Apostle Paul, is a letter of encouragement and instruction to a young church amidst persecution and trials. This epistle, one of the earliest written by Paul, addresses various aspects of Christian living and emphasizes the believer's hope in the Lord's imminent return.

Paul begins by expressing his gratitude for the Thessalonians' faith, love, and steadfastness in the face of afflictions, commending them as an example to other believers. He then reminds them of his ministry among them, characterized by integrity, affection, and a genuine desire for their spiritual growth.

A central theme of the epistle is the believer's unwavering hope in the second coming of Christ. Paul provides assurance to those who have lost loved ones, teaching that the dead in Christ will be raised first, followed by those who are alive, to meet the Lord in the air.

The letter also addresses practical matters of Christian conduct, including sexual purity, love for one another, and diligence in daily work. Paul emphasizes the importance of living in a manner that honors God and commends the gospel to unbelievers.

Throughout the epistle, Paul exhorts the Thessalonians to remain steadfast in their faith, encouraging them to persevere in prayer, rejoice always, and abstain from every form of evil. He concludes with a benediction, expressing his confidence in the Lord's faithfulness to establish and guard them until the return of Christ.

KEY EVENTS, CHARACTERS, AND TEACHINGS:

- Paul's commendation of the Thessalonians' faith, love, and steadfastness (1 Thessalonians 1:1-10)

- Paul's reminder of his ministry among them and his affection for them (1 Thessalonians 2:1-12)

- The Thessalonians' reception of the Word and their example to other believers (1 Thessalonians 2:13-16)

- Paul's longing to see the Thessalonians and his attempts to visit them (1 Thessalonians 2:17-3:13)

- Exhortations to sexual purity, brotherly love, and diligent work (1 Thessalonians 4:1-12)

- Teachings on the resurrection of the dead and the Lord's return (1 Thessalonians 4:13-5:11)

- Instructions for Christian living and conduct (1 Thessalonians 5:12-22)

EXPLORING SOME DEEPER MEANINGS:

1. The emphasis on the Thessalonians' faith, love, and hope (1 Thessalonians 1:3) reflects the essential characteristics of a thriving Christian community and the foundation for enduring afflictions.

2. Paul's example of integrity and genuine concern for the Thessalonians (1 Thessalonians 2:1-12) highlights the importance of authentic ministry and the shepherd's heart in nurturing spiritual growth.

3. The imagery of the "word of God at work" (1 Thessalonians 2:13) underscores the power of the gospel to transform lives and the responsibility of believers to receive and live out its truth.

4. The teachings on sexual purity (1 Thessalonians 4:3-8) emphasize the sacredness of the body and the importance of living in holiness, reflecting the believer's identity as a vessel for God's glory.

5. The exhortation to "lead a quiet life" and "mind your own affairs" (1 Thessalonians 4:11) encourages a lifestyle of diligence, self-discipline, and integrity in the midst of a watching world.

6. The teachings on the resurrection of the dead and the Lord's return (1 Thessalonians 4:13-5:11) provide hope and comfort for those grieving the loss of loved ones, while also emphasizing the need for watchfulness and preparedness for Christ's imminent coming.

7. The call to "rejoice always, pray without ceasing..." (1 Thessalonians 5:16-18) highlights the importance of maintaining a joyful, prayerful, and grateful attitude, even in the midst of trials and difficulties.

8. The exhortation to "abstain from every form of evil" (1 Thessalonians 5:22) underscores the believer's call to holiness and separation from the influences of the world.

9. The benediction and prayer for the Thessalonians (1 Thessalonians 5:23-24) reflect Paul's confidence in the Lord's faithfulness to sanctify and preserve His people until the return of Christ.

10. The teachings on perseverance and endurance (1 Thessalonians 3:1-5) encourage believers to remain steadfast in their faith, even in the face of opposition and persecution, trusting in God's sustaining grace

2 Thessalonians
BOOK SUMMARY:

2 Thessalonians, a letter written by the Apostle Paul to the church in Thessalonica, is a follow-up to his first epistle. This epistle aims to provide further instruction, encouragement, and clarification regarding the Second Coming of Christ and the events surrounding it.

Paul commends the Thessalonian believers for their endurance amidst persecution and their steadfast faith. He reassures them about the fate of those who have died, emphasizing that they will be resurrected at Christ's return. The apostle addresses concerns about the timing of the Second Coming, cautioning against being unsettled by false teachings or deceptions.

A significant portion of the letter focuses on the "man of lawlessness" or the Antichrist, who will arise before Christ's return. Paul warns against apostasy and exhorts the believers to stand firm in their faith and obedience to the gospel.

Throughout the epistle, Paul emphasizes the need for perseverance, diligence in work, and right living as they await the Lord's return. He encourages prayer, discipleship, and steadfastness in the face of opposition and false teachings.

2 Thessalonians reinforces the hope of Christ's return and the ultimate triumph of God's righteous judgment, while also providing practical guidance for living a life worthy of the gospel until that day arrives.

KEY EVENTS, CHARACTERS, AND TEACHINGS:

- Commendation for the Thessalonians' faith and perseverance amidst persecution

- The revelation of the "man of lawlessness" or the Antichrist

- Warnings against being deceived by false teachings about the Second Coming

- Exhortations to stand firm in the faith and obedience to the gospel

- Instructions for discipleship, prayer, and right living while awaiting Christ's return

- The fate of those who have died before Christ's return

- The timing and signs of the Second Coming and the ultimate triumph of God's righteous judgment

- Encouragement to persevere and trust in God's faithfulness and warnings against idleness and the importance of diligent work

EXPLORING SOME DEEPER MEANINGS:

1. The description of the "man of lawlessness" or the Antichrist carries symbolic significance. This figure represents the culmination of human rebellion against God and the embodiment of the spirit of lawlessness that opposes Christ's authority.

2. The concept of the "restrainer" has been interpreted in various ways, including the Holy Spirit, the Roman Empire, or a heavenly being. It symbolizes the force that holds back the full manifestation of evil until the appointed time.

3. The call to "stand firm" emphasizes the importance of perseverance and steadfastness in the face of opposition, false teachings, and the challenges of living a Christian life.

4. Paul's instructions regarding work and idleness highlight the value of diligence, self-discipline, and contributing positively to society while awaiting Christ's return.

5. The emphasis on prayer underscores the importance of intercession and spiritual support for those engaged in ministry and the spread of the gospel.

6. The reassurance about the fate of those who have died before Christ's return addresses a significant concern for the Thessalonian believers, providing hope and comfort.

7. The warnings against false teachings and deceptions surrounding the Second Coming underscore the importance of discernment and holding firmly to sound doctrine.

8. The references to the "lawless one" and the "mystery of lawlessness" suggest a cosmic conflict between the forces of good and evil, which will culminate in Christ's ultimate victory.

9. The emphasis on God's righteous judgment highlights the certainty of divine justice and the vindication of those who have endured persecution and suffering for their faith.

10. The exhortations to persevere and remain steadfast in the face of trials and opposition reflect the challenges faced by the early church and the ongoing need for endurance in the Christian life.

1 Timothy

1 Timothy is a letter written by the Apostle Paul to his beloved son in the faith, Timothy, who was serving as the pastor of the church in Ephesus. This epistle provides crucial instructions for church leadership, doctrine, and conduct within the body of Christ.

Paul's primary concern in this letter is to combat the spread of false teachings and heresies that were infiltrating the church. He emphasizes the importance of sound doctrine, godly living, and the qualifications for church leaders, such as elders and deacons.

The epistle addresses various aspects of church life, including public worship, the role of men and women in the church, and the proper treatment of widows and elders. Paul also offers guidance on handling false teachers, dealing with sin within the church, and the pursuit of godliness.

Throughout the letter, Paul underscores the centrality of the gospel message, the significance of godly character, and the call to live a life that honors Christ. He encourages Timothy to be a faithful steward of the truth, to guard the deposit of sound teaching, and to fulfill his ministry with boldness and perseverance.

1 Timothy serves as a comprehensive guide for church leadership, discipline, and the maintenance of sound doctrine, highlighting the importance of godliness, integrity, and the preservation of the gospel's purity within the Christian community.

KEY EVENTS, CHARACTERS, AND TEACHINGS:

- Instructions for church leadership and the qualifications for elders and deacons

- Warnings against false teachings and the importance of sound doctrine

- Guidance on public worship, the roles of men and women in the church, and the treatment of widows and elders

- Addressing sin and discipline within the church community

- The centrality of the gospel message and the pursuit of godliness

- Encouragement for Timothy to fulfill his ministry faithfully and persevere in the face of challenges

- The significance of godly character and living a life that honors Christ

- The importance of guarding the deposit of sound teaching and preserving the purity of the gospel

EXPLORING SOME DEEPER MEANINGS:

1. The qualifications for elders and deacons (1 Timothy 3:1-13) emphasize the importance of godly character, integrity, and spiritual maturity in church leadership. These qualifications reflect the high standards expected of those entrusted with the care and oversight of God's people.

2. The warnings against false teachings (1 Timothy 1:3-7; 4:1-5; 6:3-5) highlight the ongoing battle against heresies and distortions of the truth. Paul's admonitions underscore the need for vigilance and a firm commitment to sound doctrine in the face of deceptive teachings.

3. The instructions concerning public worship (1 Timothy 2:1-15) provide guidance on prayer, the roles of men and women, and the importance of living a life of godliness and submission to authority. These teachings reflect the cultural context while upholding biblical principles.

4. The instructions regarding the treatment of widows (1 Timothy 5:3-16) demonstrate the church's responsibility to care for the vulnerable and honor those who have served faithfully. These instructions also highlight the importance of family responsibilities and the need for discernment in addressing potential abuses.

5. The warnings against the love of money and the pursuit of wealth (1 Timothy 6:6-10, 17-19) underscore the dangers of materialism and the importance of contentment, generosity, and storing up treasures in heaven.

6. The emphasis on godliness and the pursuit of righteousness (1 Timothy 4:7-8; 6:11-12) highlights the centrality of spiritual disciplines and the cultivation of a life that reflects the character of Christ.

7. The instructions on addressing sin within the church (1 Timothy 5:19-22) provide guidance on handling accusations against elders and the need for impartiality and due process in matters of discipline.

8. The references to the "mystery of godliness" (1 Timothy 3:16) and the "good confession" (1 Timothy 6:12-13) point to the profound truths of the Christian faith and the call to hold firmly to the gospel message.

9. The exhortations to Timothy to "fight the good fight" (1 Timothy 1:18-19; 6:12) and to "guard the deposit" (1 Timothy 6:20) emphasize the importance of perseverance, faithfulness, and the preservation of sound teaching in the face of opposition and challenges.

10. The warnings against vain discussions and controversies (1 Timothy 1:4; 6:4-5) highlight the need to avoid fruitless debates and instead focus on promoting godliness, faith, and love within the church community.

2 Timothy

BOOK SUMMARY:

2 Timothy is a deeply personal letter written by the Apostle Paul to his beloved son in the faith, Timothy, during Paul's final imprisonment in Rome. This epistle serves as a poignant farewell and a solemn charge to Timothy, encouraging him to remain steadfast in the faith and to carry on the legacy of sound doctrine and ministry.

In this letter, Paul expresses his profound affection for Timothy and his confidence in him as a faithful minister of the gospel. He reminds Timothy of the gift of God's grace and the importance of fanning into flame the spiritual gifts bestowed upon him.

A central theme of 2 Timothy is the endurance of suffering for the sake of the gospel. Paul shares his own experiences of persecution and hardship, exhorting Timothy to embrace the same spirit of endurance and to be prepared to face opposition and trials.

The epistle emphasizes the importance of sound doctrine, warning against false teachers and the dangers of apostasy. Paul urges Timothy to hold firm to the truth of the gospel, to preach the Word with boldness, and to entrust the teachings to faithful men who can pass them on to future generations.

Throughout the letter, Paul reflects on his life and ministry, expressing gratitude for those who have supported him and offering words of encouragement and guidance to Timothy. He reminds him of the power of the Scriptures and the necessity of being a diligent worker, rightly handling the Word of truth.

2 Timothy serves as a powerful testament to the unwavering commitment required in ministry, the value of godly mentorship, and the call to persevere in the face of adversity, all while keeping the faith and proclaiming the gospel with unwavering conviction.

KEY EVENTS, CHARACTERS, AND TEACHINGS:

- Paul's affirmation of Timothy's faith and calling to ministry

- Exhortations to endure suffering and hardship for the sake of the gospel

- Warnings against false teachers, apostasy, and the dangers of godless living

- The importance of sound doctrine, preaching the Word, and entrusting the teachings to faithful men

- Paul's reflections on his life, ministry, and impending martyrdom

- The power and sufficiency of the Scriptures for equipping believers

- The call to be a diligent worker, rightly handling the Word of truth

- The necessity of perseverance, steadfastness, and remaining faithful to the end

EXPLORING SOME DEEPER MEANINGS:

1. The metaphor of a "good soldier of Christ Jesus" (2 Timothy 2:3-4) highlights the sacrificial nature of ministry and the call to endure hardship, remain focused on the mission, and avoid entanglements with worldly affairs.

2. The imagery of a "vessel for honor" (2 Timothy 2:20-21) emphasizes the importance of personal holiness, purity of heart, and being set apart for God's purposes, ready for every good work.

3. The warnings against "quarreling about words" (2 Timothy 2:14) and "foolish and stupid arguments" (2 Timothy 2:23) underscore the need to avoid fruitless debates and controversies that lead to division and distract from the pursuit of godliness.

4. The description of the last days as "perilous times" (2 Timothy 3:1-9) and the portrayal of godless people with corrupted minds and counterfeit faith serve as a sobering reminder of the spiritual battles believers face and the importance of remaining steadfast in the truth.

5. The reference to the Scriptures as "God-breathed" (2 Timothy 3:16) affirms their divine inspiration and authority, highlighting their sufficiency for teaching, rebuking, correcting, and training in righteousness.

6. The exhortation to "preach the word" (2 Timothy 4:2) and the urgency to proclaim the gospel in season and out of season emphasize the primacy of preaching and the responsibility of ministers to be faithful heralds of the truth.

7. The imagery of "fighting the good fight" and "finishing the race" (2 Timothy 4:7) reflects the perseverance required in ministry and the commitment to remain faithful until the end, regardless of the challenges faced.

8. The reference to the "crown of righteousness" (2 Timothy 4:8) represents the reward awaiting those who have faithfully served Christ and longed for His appearing, highlighting the eternal perspective and hope that sustains believers.

9. The mention of deserters like Demas (2 Timothy 4:10) and opposers like Alexander the metalworker (2 Timothy 4:14-15) serve as cautionary tales, reminding readers of the reality of spiritual warfare and the need to remain vigilant against compromises and opposition.

10. The emphasis on passing on the teachings to "faithful men" (2 Timothy 2:2) underscores the importance of discipleship, mentorship, and the generational transmission of sound doctrine, ensuring the continuity of the gospel message.

Titus

BOOK SUMMARY:

The Epistle of Paul to Titus is a concise yet profound letter written by the Apostle Paul to his co-worker Titus, who was overseeing the churches on the island of Crete. This epistle serves as a guide for establishing order, sound doctrine, and godly leadership within the Christian communities.

Paul's primary concern in this letter is to address the challenges faced by the churches in Crete, which were plagued by false teachers, rebellion, and moral laxity. He instructs Titus on the qualifications and responsibilities of elders, emphasizing the need for godly character, sound doctrine, and effective teaching.

The epistle highlights the importance of living a life that adorns the doctrine of God, with specific instructions for various groups within the church, such as older men and women, younger men and women, and slaves. Paul emphasizes the transformative power of the gospel and the necessity of good works as evidence of genuine faith.

Throughout the letter, Paul underscores the centrality of sound doctrine, the need for godly living, and the importance of maintaining good deeds and submission to authority. He exhorts Titus to refute those who oppose sound teaching and to rebuke sharply those who disrupt the unity of the church.

The Epistle to Titus serves as a practical guide for church leadership, discipline, and the preservation of sound doctrine. It emphasizes the inseparable connection between right belief and right living, calling believers to reflect the grace of God in their daily conduct and relationships.

KEY EVENTS, CHARACTERS, AND TEACHINGS:

- Instructions for appointing qualified elders with godly character and sound doctrine

- Warnings against false teachers and the importance of maintaining sound doctrine

- Guidance for godly living and good works that adorn the doctrine of God

- Specific instructions for various groups within the church (older men, older women, younger men, younger women, slaves)

- The transformative power of the gospel and the necessity of good works as evidence of genuine faith

- Exhortations to refute those who oppose sound teaching and maintain unity within the church

- The centrality of sound doctrine and the inseparable connection between right belief and right living

EXPLORING SOME DEEPER MEANINGS:

1. The qualifications for elders (Titus 1:5-9) emphasize the importance of godly character, self-control, and the ability to teach sound doctrine, reflecting the high standards expected of church leaders.

2. The warnings against "rebellious people, mere talkers and deceivers" (Titus 1:10-16) highlight the dangers of false teachings and the need for discernment and firm adherence to the truth.

3. The instructions for older men and women (Titus 2:1-5) underscore the importance of godly mentorship, modeling virtue, and the transmission of sound doctrine through discipleship.

4. The exhortations for younger men and women (Titus 2:6-8) emphasize the need for self-control, purity, and living in a way that brings honor to the gospel and silences critics.

5. The instructions for slaves (Titus 2:9-10) reflect the cultural context while promoting principles of integrity, respect for authority, and the adornment of the gospel through faithful service.

6. The statement "the grace of God that brings salvation has appeared to all" (Titus 2:11) highlights the universality of God's saving grace and the transformative power of the gospel.

7. The concept of "denying ungodliness and worldly lusts" and "living soberly, righteously, and godly" (Titus 2:12-13) emphasizes the practical implications of the gospel in daily life and the call to pursue holiness.

8. The description of Christ's sacrifice "to redeem us from every lawless deed and purify for Himself His own special people" (Titus 2:14) underscores the purpose of redemption and the identity of believers as God's treasured possession.

9. The emphasis on "being ready for every good work" (Titus 3:1) highlights the importance of practical service and the outworking of faith through good deeds.

10. The exhortation to "avoid foolish disputes, genealogies, contentions, and strivings about the law" (Titus 3:9) reflects the need to avoid fruitless debates and controversies that distract from the pursuit of godliness and unity.

Philemon
BOOK SUMMARY:

The Epistle of Paul to Philemon is a personal letter written by the Apostle Paul to Philemon, a beloved fellow believer and leader in the church at Colossae. This short epistle addresses a delicate situation involving Philemon's runaway slave, Onesimus, and serves as a powerful illustration of the transformative power of the gospel and the principles of Christian reconciliation and forgiveness.

In the letter, Paul appeals to Philemon to receive Onesimus, who had become a believer under Paul's ministry, not merely as a slave but as a beloved brother in Christ. Paul's approach is one of gentle persuasion, acknowledging Philemon's rights as a slave owner while emphasizing the higher calling of Christian love and unity.

The epistle highlights the equalizing effect of the gospel, where distinctions of social status and background are transcended by the common bond of faith in Christ. Paul skillfully employs rhetorical devices and a tone of affection to appeal to Philemon's sense of Christian compassion and his willingness to forgive and reconcile with Onesimus.

Throughout the letter, Paul underscores the principles of grace, forgiveness, and the restoration of broken relationships. He offers to take personal responsibility for any wrongdoing on Onesimus's part and expresses his desire for Philemon to receive Onesimus as he would receive Paul himself.

The Epistle to Philemon serves as a powerful reminder of the transformative impact of the gospel on human relationships and the call to extend grace, forgiveness, and acceptance to those who have been reconciled to Christ, regardless of their past or social standing.

KEY EVENTS, CHARACTERS, AND TEACHINGS:

- The characters of Paul, Philemon, Onesimus, and their relationships

- Paul's appeal for Philemon to receive Onesimus as a brother in Christ

- The transformative power of the gospel in transcending social divisions

- The principles of Christian reconciliation, forgiveness, and restoration

- The equalizing effect of the gospel, where believers are united in Christ

- Paul's offer to take personal responsibility for Onesimus's wrongdoing

- The emphasis on grace, compassion, and willingness to forgive and reconcile

- The call to extend acceptance and love to those reconciled to Christ

- The impact of the gospel on transforming human relationships

- The rhetorical strategies and tone of persuasion employed by Paul

EXPLORING SOME DEEPER MEANINGS:

1. The description of Onesimus as "once unprofitable, but now profitable" (Philemon 1:11) highlights the transformative power of the gospel and the new identity believers receive in Christ.

2. Paul's use of the term "brother" (Philemon 1:16) to describe Onesimus underscores the equalizing effect of the gospel, where social distinctions are transcended by the bond of faith in Christ.

3. The metaphor of Onesimus as Paul's "child" (Philemon 1:10) reflects the spiritual relationship between Paul and those he led to Christ, emphasizing the bonds of spiritual kinship that supersede earthly ties.

4. Paul's statement, "If he has wronged you or owes anything, put that on my account" (Philemon 1:18), demonstrates his willingness to take personal responsibility for Onesimus's actions and reflects the principle of substitutionary sacrifice.

5. The reference to Philemon's "love and faith toward the Lord Jesus and toward all the saints" (Philemon 1:5) highlights the importance of expressing genuine Christian love and unity within the body of Christ.

6. Paul's appeal to Philemon "for love's sake" (Philemon 1:9) emphasizes the centrality of love in Christian relationships and the call to extend grace and forgiveness to one another.

7. The phrase "that you might receive him forever" (Philemon 1:15) suggests the permanence of the reconciliation and restoration sought by Paul, reflecting the enduring nature of Christian fellowship.

8. Paul's statement, "I did not want to do anything without your consent" (Philemon 1:14), demonstrates his respect for Philemon's authority and his desire for voluntary cooperation rooted in love.

9. The mention of Philemon's "refreshing the hearts of the saints" (Philemon 1:7) highlights the impact of Christian hospitality and the importance of encouraging and uplifting fellow believers.

10. Paul's expression of confidence in Philemon's obedience (Philemon 1:21) reflects his trust in the transformative power of the gospel to shape believers' attitudes and actions.

Hebrews

BOOK SUMMARY:

The Epistle to the Hebrews is a profound and eloquent treatise that presents the supremacy of Jesus Christ and the superiority of the New Covenant over the Old Covenant. While the author remains anonymous, the letter is addressed to Jewish believers who were facing persecution and the temptation to revert to their former religious practices.

The epistle begins by establishing the preeminence of Christ as the final and ultimate revelation of God, superior to the prophets and angels. It then proceeds to demonstrate Christ's superiority over Moses, the high priests, and the sacrificial system of the Old Covenant.

A central theme of Hebrews is the concept of Christ as the great High Priest, who offered Himself as the perfect and eternal sacrifice for sin. The author emphasizes the inadequacy of the Old Covenant sacrifices and the finality of Christ's sacrifice, which opens the way for believers to have direct access to God.

Throughout the epistle, the author exhorts the readers to persevere in their faith, warning against the dangers of unbelief and apostasy. They are encouraged to hold fast to the hope they profess, to draw near to God with confidence, and to spur one another on toward love and good deeds.

The book of Hebrews also presents a rich tapestry of examples from the Old Testament, showcasing the heroes of faith who persevered despite trials and adversity. These examples serve as inspiration for believers to endure and remain faithful to the end.

Ultimately, Hebrews proclaims the superiority of the New Covenant, the finality of Christ's sacrifice, and the call to live a life of faith, obedience, and perseverance, with an unwavering hope in the promises of God.

KEY EVENTS, CHARACTERS, AND TEACHINGS:

- The supremacy and preeminence of Jesus Christ as the final revelation of God

- The superiority of Christ over prophets, angels, Moses, and the Old Covenant priesthood

- Christ as the great High Priest, offering Himself as the perfect and eternal sacrifice

- The inadequacy of the Old Covenant sacrifices and the finality of Christ's sacrifice

- Direct access to God through Christ's sacrifice and the New Covenant

- Exhortations to persevere in faith, hold fast to hope, and spur one another on

- Warnings against unbelief, apostasy, and neglecting salvation

- The heroes of faith from the Old Testament as examples of endurance

- The superiority of the New Covenant and the call to obedience and faithfulness

- The promise of an unshakable kingdom and the need for reverence and worship

EXPLORING SOME DEEPER MEANINGS:

1. The description of Christ as the "radiance of God's glory and the exact representation of His being" (Hebrews 1:3) highlights Christ's divine nature and His unique role as the perfect revelation of God.

2. The concept of Christ as the "pioneer and perfecter of our faith" (Hebrews 12:2) emphasizes His leadership and example in the journey of faith, as well as His role in bringing it to completion.

3. The metaphor of the "anchor for the soul" (Hebrews 6:19) represents the steadfastness and security found in the hope believers have in Christ, which anchors them amidst life's storms.

4. The description of the Old Covenant as a "shadow of the good things to come" (Hebrews 10:1) underscores its temporary and symbolic nature, pointing forward to the reality and fulfillment found in Christ.

5. The concept of the "new and living way" (Hebrews 10:20) refers to the direct access to God made possible through Christ's sacrifice, in contrast to the restricted access of the Old Covenant.

6. The imagery of the "heavenly country" (Hebrews 11:16) and the "city with foundations" (Hebrews 11:10) represents the eternal inheritance and the ultimate fulfillment of God's promises for believers.

7. The exhortation to "lay aside every weight and the sin that so easily entangles" (Hebrews 12:1) emphasizes the need for perseverance in the Christian life by removing hindrances and distractions.

8. The reference to the "discipline of the Lord" (Hebrews 12:5-11) highlights God's loving correction and training of His children, which leads to holiness and righteousness.

9. The warning against "failing to reach the promised rest" (Hebrews 4:1) underscores the importance of persevering in faith and not neglecting the salvation offered in Christ.

10. The description of Christ as the "mediator of a new covenant" (Hebrews 9:15) emphasizes His role as the intermediary between God and humanity, establishing a new and superior covenant.

11. The concept of "boldness to enter the holy places" (Hebrews 10:19) refers to the confidence and access believers have through Christ's sacrifice, enabling them to approach God's presence.

12. The admonition to "not neglect meeting together" (Hebrews 10:25) highlights the importance of Christian fellowship and encouraging one another in the face of trials and persecution.

13. The examples of the heroes of faith from the Old Testament (Hebrews 11) serve as inspiration and encouragement for believers to persevere in their faith, even in the face of adversity and hardship.

14. The description of God's word as "living and active, sharper than any double-edged sword" (Hebrews 4:12) emphasizes the power and penetrating nature of Scripture in discerning the thoughts and intentions of the heart.

15. The exhortation to "run with endurance the race set before us" (Hebrews 12:1) highlights the need for perseverance and steadfastness in the Christian life, keeping our eyes fixed on Jesus.

James
BOOK SUMMARY:

The Epistle of James is a highly practical and wisdom-filled letter written by James, the half-brother of Jesus and a leader in the early church. This epistle addresses a diverse audience of Jewish believers dispersed throughout the Roman world, offering guidance on living out genuine faith in the midst of trials and temptations.

James emphasizes the importance of putting faith into action and the need for a consistent, moral lifestyle that reflects the teachings of Christ. He addresses various aspects of Christian living, such as perseverance, wisdom, speech, favoritism, works, and prayer.

A central theme of the epistle is the relationship between faith and works. James challenges the notion of a mere intellectual assent to the faith, insisting that true faith must be evidenced by good deeds and a transformed life. He provides numerous examples of how faith should manifest itself in practical ways, such as caring for the poor, controlling the tongue, and exercising patience in trials.

Throughout the letter, James exhorts believers to be doers of the Word and not merely hearers, highlighting the importance of obedience and the futility of self-deception. He addresses issues of temptation, the role of the tongue in controlling one's conduct, and the need for humility and wisdom from above.

The Epistle of James serves as a powerful reminder that genuine faith is not merely a matter of intellectual assent but rather a living, active expression of God's transforming work in the lives of believers. It challenges readers to embody the teachings of Christ in their daily lives, reflecting the wisdom and maturity that come from an authentic relationship with God.

KEY EVENTS, CHARACTERS, AND TEACHINGS:

- The author, James, the half-brother of Jesus and a leader in the early church

- The emphasis on the need for perseverance and steadfastness in the face of trials

- The relationship between faith and works, and the necessity of demonstrating faith through actions

- The importance of being doers of the Word and not merely hearers

- The role of wisdom, humility, and prayer in the life of a believer

- The control of the tongue and the power of speech

- The danger of showing favoritism and the call for impartial love

- The critique of dead faith and the examples of living faith through good deeds

- The warnings against worldliness, quarreling, and the misuse of wealth

- The call to patience, endurance, and prayer in the midst of suffering

- The exhortations to confess sins, pray for one another, and restore wandering believers

- The overarching theme of living out genuine, active faith in daily life

EXPLORING SOME DEEPER MEANINGS:

1. The concept of "pure and undefiled religion" (James 1:27) emphasizes the importance of caring for the vulnerable and remaining unstained by the world, reflecting true spiritual devotion.

2. The metaphor of being "a mirror of the Word" (James 1:23-25) highlights the need for self-examination and the application of Scripture to one's life, rather than merely hearing and forgetting.

3. The description of the "perfect law, the law of liberty" (James 1:25) refers to the gospel of Christ and the freedom it provides from the bondage of sin and legalism.

4. The warning against being "double-minded" (James 1:8) reflects the need for spiritual integrity and consistency, avoiding a divided allegiance between God and the world.

5. The comparison of the tongue to a "fire" and a "world of iniquity" (James 3:6) underscores the power of speech to influence and corrupt, and the need for self-control and wisdom.

6. The imagery of "bitter envy and self-seeking" (James 3:14-16) represents the destructive nature of worldly wisdom and the antithesis of the humility and peace that characterize true wisdom from above.

7. The admonition against showing "partiality" or "favoritism" (James 2:1-9) highlights the need for impartial love and the rejection of discrimination based on outward appearances or social status.

8. The concept of "faith without works is dead" (James 2:17) emphasizes the inseparable connection between genuine faith and its practical outworking through good deeds and obedience. With examples of Abraham and Rahab (James 2:21-26) illustrates how faith is made complete and justified by actions.

9. The warnings against worldliness, quarreling, and the misuse of wealth (James 4:1-5:6) address the dangers of being influenced by ungodly desires and the pursuit of material gain at the expense of spiritual priorities.

10. The call to patience, endurance, and prayer in the midst of suffering (James 5:7-11) encourages believers to follow the example of the prophets and Job, trusting in God's sovereign purposes and the promise of Christ's return.

11. The exhortations to confess sins, pray for one another, and restore wandering believers (James 5:16-20) highlight the importance of accountability, intercessory prayer, and the responsibility of the church community to care for one another.

12. The concept of "pure religion" being to "visit orphans and widows in their affliction" (James 1:27) reflects the call to practical, compassionate service and care for the vulnerable and marginalized.

13. The admonition against being "a friend of the world" (James 4:4) highlights the incompatibility of worldly values and desires with true devotion to God, calling for a clear separation and allegiance to Christ.

1 Peter
BOOK SUMMARY:

The First Epistle of Peter is a profound and encouraging letter written by the Apostle Peter to believers who were facing intense persecution and suffering for their faith. Peter, one of the closest disciples of Jesus, writes to offer comfort, hope, and practical instructions for living as faithful followers of Christ in the midst of trials.

Peter begins by reminding the believers of their living hope in Christ, their secure inheritance, and the genuineness of their faith, which is being tested and refined through various trials. He emphasizes the privileged position they hold as God's chosen people, called to proclaim the praises of Him who called them out of darkness into His marvelous light.

A central theme of the epistle is the call to live as strangers and aliens in this world, maintaining holy conduct and demonstrating Christ-like character in all aspects of life. Peter provides practical guidance on how to live as faithful witnesses, whether in the context of marriage, the workplace, or society at large.

Throughout the letter, Peter exhorts believers to endure suffering with patience and joy, following the example of Christ, who suffered unjustly for their sake. He encourages them to arm themselves with the same mindset as Christ, rejecting sinful desires and living for the will of God.

The epistle also addresses the responsibilities of church leaders and the importance of humility, submission to authority, and love for one another within the community of believers. Peter emphasizes the need for steadfastness, watchfulness, and resistance against the schemes of the devil.

Ultimately, 1 Peter is a powerful call to embrace the sufferings of Christ while maintaining a fervent hope in the glory that will be revealed, living as faithful witnesses in a hostile world, and entrusting their souls to the faithful Creator.

KEY EVENTS, CHARACTERS, AND TEACHINGS:

- The author, Peter, one of the closest disciples of Jesus and a leader in the early church

- The recipients, believers facing persecution and suffering for their faith

- The emphasis on the living hope in Christ and the secure inheritance awaiting believers

- The call to live as strangers and aliens in this world, maintaining holy conduct and Christ-like character

- The exhortations to endure suffering with patience and joy, following the example of Christ

- The instructions on living as faithful witnesses in various spheres of life (marriage, workplace, society)

- The responsibilities of church leaders and the importance of humility, submission, and love within the church

- The need for steadfastness, watchfulness, and resistance against the schemes of the devil

- The encouragement to entrust their souls to the faithful Creator, even in the midst of trials

- The hope in the glory that will be revealed and the call to embrace the sufferings of Christ

- The instructions for holy living, including rejecting sinful desires and living for the will of God

- The call to be sober-minded, watchful, and fervent in prayer

- The emphasis on the privileged position of believers as God's chosen people, called to proclaim His praises

- The importance of maintaining unity, hospitality, and using spiritual gifts to serve one another

EXPLORING SOME DEEPER MEANINGS:

1. The imagery of being "born again to a living hope" (1 Peter 1:3) represents the transformative power of salvation and the new life believers have in Christ, marked by a confident expectation of their eternal inheritance.

2. The description of believers as "sojourners and pilgrims" (1 Peter 2:11) highlights their temporary status in this world and the need to maintain a heavenly perspective, living as faithful witnesses amidst a hostile culture.

3. The metaphor of being "living stones" being built into a "spiritual house" (1 Peter 2:5) emphasizes the corporate identity of believers as the dwelling place of God's Spirit and their role in proclaiming His praises.

4. The concept of the "precious cornerstone" (1 Peter 2:6-8) refers to Christ, the foundation upon which the church is built, and the stumbling block for those who reject His authority.

5. The exhortation to "abstain from fleshly lusts which wage war against the soul" (1 Peter 2:11) underscores the ongoing spiritual battle against sinful desires and the need for vigilance and self-control.

6. The call to "arm yourselves with the same mindset as Christ" (1 Peter 4:1) encourages believers to adopt the attitude of willingness to suffer for doing good, following in the footsteps of Christ's example.

7. The description of the "living word of God" (1 Peter 1:23) highlights the power of the gospel message and its ability to bring about spiritual rebirth and transformation.

8. The metaphor of being "a royal priesthood" (1 Peter 2:9) emphasizes the privileged position of believers as ministers of God's grace, offering spiritual sacrifices and proclaiming His praises.

9. The instruction for wives to be submissive to their husbands (1 Peter 3:1-6) is contextualized within the cultural norms of the time and emphasizes the witness of a gentle and respectful spirit, even in the face of an unbelieving spouse.

10. The admonition for husbands to honor their wives (1 Peter 3:7) highlights the need for mutual respect and understanding within marriage, treating wives as co-heirs of the grace of life.

11. The call to "love the brotherhood" (1 Peter 2:17) underscores the importance of genuine love and unity within the community of believers, reflecting the character of Christ.

12. The instructions for elders to shepherd the flock willingly and with humility (1 Peter 5:1-4) emphasize the responsibility of church leaders to serve as examples of

Christ-like leadership and care for the spiritual well-being of the believers.

13. The exhortation to "humble yourselves under the mighty hand of God" (1 Peter 5:6) encourages believers to embrace a posture of submission and trust in God's sovereign timing and purposes, particularly in times of suffering.

14. The warning against the "roaring lion" (1 Peter 5:8) highlights the reality of spiritual warfare and the need for vigilance, resistance, and steadfastness in the faith, relying on God's grace and strength.

15. The emphasis on "the true grace of God" (1 Peter 5:12) and the call to "stand firm in it" underscores the sufficiency of God's grace and the importance of persevering in the face of trials, anchored in the truth of the gospel.

2 Peter

BOOK SUMMARY:

The Second Epistle of Peter is a powerful and urgent letter written by the Apostle Peter near the end of his life. This epistle serves as a passionate call to the church to maintain sound doctrine, resist false teachers, and grow in the grace and knowledge of Jesus Christ.

Peter begins by reminding believers of the genuine faith they share and the divine power that has been granted to them through the knowledge of Christ. He exhorts them to make every effort to supplement their faith with virtues such as moral excellence, knowledge, self-control, perseverance, godliness, brotherly kindness, and love.

A significant portion of the epistle is dedicated to warning against false teachers who distort the truth and introduce destructive heresies. Peter vividly describes the characteristics of these deceivers, their exploitation of others, and the certainty of their judgment. He calls for vigilance and steadfastness in the true knowledge of Christ.

Throughout the letter, Peter emphasizes the trustworthiness of the prophetic word and the eyewitness accounts of Christ's majesty, affirming the divine inspiration of Scripture. He reminds believers of the certainty of Christ's return and the coming judgment, exhorting them to live holy and godly lives as they await the day of the Lord.

The epistle also addresses the scoffers who mock the promise of Christ's return, affirming the trustworthiness of God's word and the reality of His patience, which allows time for repentance. Peter encourages believers to grow in the grace and knowledge of the Lord Jesus Christ, warning against being led astray by the error of the wicked.

Ultimately, 2 Peter is a powerful exhortation to remain steadfast in the true knowledge of Christ, reject false teachings, and diligently pursue spiritual growth, living in eager anticipation of the day of the Lord.

KEY EVENTS, CHARACTERS, AND TEACHINGS:

- The author, Peter, one of the closest disciples of Jesus and a leader in the early church

- The emphasis on the genuine faith shared by believers and the divine power granted through the knowledge of Christ

- The exhortation to supplement faith with virtues such as moral excellence, knowledge, self-control, perseverance, godliness, brotherly kindness, and love

- The warnings against false teachers, their characteristics, exploitation, and the certainty of their judgment

- The call for vigilance and steadfastness in the true knowledge of Christ

- The affirmation of the trustworthiness of the prophetic word and the divine inspiration of Scripture

- The reminders of the certainty of Christ's return and the coming judgment

- The exhortations to live holy and godly lives in anticipation of the day of the Lord

- The refutation of scoffers who mock the promise of Christ's return, affirming God's patience for repentance

- The encouragement to grow in the grace and knowledge of the Lord Jesus Christ, avoiding being led astray by error

- The emphasis on the prophetic word as a lamp shining in a dark place until the dawning of the day

- The description of the transfiguration as an eyewitness account of Christ's majesty

- The affirmation of the divine origin and trustworthiness of Scripture through the inspiration of the Holy Spirit

EXPLORING SOME DEEPER MEANINGS:

1. The description of believers receiving a "faith of the same kind as ours" (2 Peter 1:1) highlights the unity and equality of all believers in the shared faith and the divine inheritance.

2. The exhortation to "make every effort to supplement your faith" (2 Peter 1:5-7) underscores the active role believers play in their spiritual growth and the importance of cultivating virtues that lead to a fruitful and effective life in Christ.

3. The imagery of being "blind or short-sighted" (2 Peter 1:9) represents the spiritual blindness and lack of perspective that results from failing to grow in the knowledge of Christ and pursue holiness.

4. The metaphor of the "prophetic word as a lamp shining in a dark place" (2 Peter 1:19) emphasizes the guiding light of Scripture in a world of spiritual darkness and the certainty of its fulfillment.

5. The description of false teachers as "waterless springs and mists driven by a storm" (2 Peter 2:17) highlights their emptiness, deception, and the futility of their teachings.

6. The portrayal of false teachers as "promising freedom while they themselves are slaves of depravity" (2 Peter 2:19) underscores their hypocrisy and the bondage they are in to their own sinful desires.

7. The analogy of the "dog returning to its vomit" and the "sow, after washing, wallowing in the mire" (2 Peter 2:22) vividly depicts the wretched condition of those who have known the truth but turned away from it.

8. The concept of God's "patience" (2 Peter 3:9) highlights His merciful desire for all to come to repentance, even as scoffers mock the delay of Christ's return.

9. The description of the "day of the Lord" as a "thief in the night" (2 Peter 3:10) emphasizes the suddenness and unexpectedness of Christ's return and the need for constant readiness.

10. The imagery of the "heavens passing away with a roar and the elements being destroyed with intense heat" (2 Peter 3:10-12) underscores the cataclysmic nature of the coming judgment and the dissolution of the present world order.

11. The promise of "new heavens and a new earth, in which righteousness dwells" (2 Peter 3:13) represents the hope of a renewed creation free from the corruption and consequences of sin.

12. The admonition to be "diligent to be found by Him in peace, spotless and blameless" (2 Peter 3:14) highlights the need for holy living and blameless conduct as we await the day of the Lord.

13. The affirmation of Paul's writings as "Scripture" (2 Peter 3:16) confirms the divine inspiration and authority of the apostolic writings, equating them with the Old Testament prophets.

14. The warning against being "led astray by the error of the wicked" (2 Peter 3:17) underscores the danger of being drawn away from the truth and the need for vigilance and steadfastness in the faith.

15. The exhortation to "grow in the grace and knowledge of our Lord and Savior Jesus Christ" (2 Peter 3:18) emphasizes the ongoing pursuit of spiritual growth, deepening our understanding of Christ, and experiencing the fullness of His grace.

1 John
BOOK SUMMARY:

The First Epistle of John, authored by the apostle John, is a profound and intimate letter that addresses the essence of Christian life and fellowship with God. Written towards the end of the first century, this epistle serves as a rich theological treatise and a practical guide for the early church, offering timeless wisdom and encouragement to believers of all ages.

John's primary emphasis is on the centrality of love – love for God and love for one another. He underscores the importance of obedience to God's commandments, which is the true expression of love, and warns against false teachings that threatened the spiritual well-being of the church. Throughout the epistle, John highlights the assurance of salvation, the forgiveness of sins, and the victory over the world through faith in Jesus Christ.

The epistle begins with a powerful affirmation of the incarnation of Christ, the Word of Life, who was manifested in human form. John declares that he and the other apostles were eyewitnesses to this profound truth, providing a firsthand testimony to the reality of Christ's life, death, and resurrection.

As the letter progresses, John expounds on the themes of light and darkness, truth and falsehood, love and hatred, emphasizing the necessity of walking in the light of God's truth and embracing a life of obedience and righteousness. He contrasts the children of God with the children of the devil, urging believers to remain steadfast in the faith and reject the worldly influences that seek to undermine their relationship with God.

John also addresses the issue of sin, assuring believers that if they confess their sins, God is faithful and just to forgive them and cleanse them from all unrighteousness. He encourages believers to maintain a life of purity, rejecting the ways of the world and pursuing holiness through the power of the indwelling Holy Spirit.

Towards the end of the epistle, John exhorts his readers to test the spirits, discerning true doctrine from false teachings, and to love one another as a mark of genuine faith. He emphasizes the assurance of eternal life for those who believe in the Son of God and encourages believers to have confidence in their relationship with God.

Overall, the First Epistle of John is a powerful reminder of the transformative power of God's love, the necessity of obedience to His commandments, and the importance of maintaining fellowship with Him and with one another. It challenges believers to live authentic lives that reflect the light of Christ and to stand firm against the deceptions of the world.

KEY EVENTS, CHARACTERS, AND TEACHINGS:

- The affirmation of the incarnation of the Word of Life (Jesus Christ) and the apostolic eyewitness testimony (1 John 1:1-4)

- The contrast between light and darkness, truth and falsehood, emphasizing the need to walk in the light (1 John 1:5-2:11)

- The assurance of forgiveness and cleansing from sin through confession and obedience (1 John 1:9, 2:1-2)

- The command to love one another as children of God (1 John 2:7-11, 3:11-18, 4:7-21)

- The warning against false teachers and the importance of discernment (1 John 2:18-27, 4:1-6)

- The promise of eternal life for those who believe in the Son of God (1 John 5:11-13)

- The confidence and assurance of answered prayer according to God's will (1 John 5:14-15)

EXPLORING SOME DEEPER MEANINGS:

1. The imagery of light and darkness is a recurring metaphor throughout the epistle, representing truth and falsehood, righteousness and sin. John urges believers to walk in the light, living according to God's truth and avoiding the deceptions of darkness.

2. The concept of "fellowship" carries profound spiritual significance, referring not only to the community of believers but also to the intimate relationship with God made possible through Christ. John emphasizes the importance of maintaining this fellowship through obedience and love.

3. The term "antichrist" is used symbolically to represent any false teaching or ideology that denies the deity and incarnation of Christ. John warns against the spirit of the antichrist, which seeks to deceive and lead believers astray.

4. The concept of "anointing" refers to the indwelling presence of the Holy Spirit, who guides believers into all truth and enables them to discern false teachings. John encourages believers to rely on this anointing for spiritual insight and understanding.

5. The emphasis on "overcoming the world" signifies the victory of faith over the temptations and influences of the world system that stands in opposition to God. John exhorts believers to remain steadfast in their faith and not succumb to the allure of worldly desires.

6. The command to "love one another" is a central theme throughout the epistle. John presents love as the ultimate expression of obedience to God and the distinguishing mark of true believers. He contrasts this love with the hatred and selfishness of the world.

7. The concept of "eternal life" is not merely a future reality but a present possession for those who believe in Christ. John assures believers of the certainty of their salvation and encourages them to live with confidence in their relationship with God.

8. The admonition to "test the spirits" highlights the importance of discernment and the ability to distinguish true doctrine from false teachings. John provides criteria for identifying the Spirit of God, such as the confession of Christ's incarnation and obedience to God's commandments.

9. The emphasis on "abiding" in Christ and in His love underscores the necessity of maintaining a close, enduring relationship with God through obedience and faithfulness. John presents abiding as the key to bearing spiritual fruit and experiencing the fullness of God's blessings.

2 John

BOOK SUMMARY:

The Second Epistle of John, a brief yet profound letter, is believed to have been written by the apostle John to a specific church congregation, often referred to as "the elect lady and her children." This epistle serves as a powerful exhortation to remain steadfast in the truth of Christ's teachings, while also emphasizing the importance of love and obedience to God's commandments.

In this concise epistle, John reaffirms the centrality of Christ's incarnation, a doctrine that was being challenged by false teachers during that time. He warns against those who deny this fundamental truth and urges believers to guard themselves against such deceptive teachings. John emphasizes the importance of walking in the truth, as they have received it from the beginning, and maintaining unwavering allegiance to the apostolic doctrine.

A recurring theme throughout the epistle is the command to love one another. John presents love as the highest expression of obedience to God's commandments, and he cautions against association with those who propagate false doctrines, as such association could undermine the believers' faithful witness.

John also addresses the issue of hospitality, encouraging believers to extend warmth and kindness to fellow believers who are traveling and teaching the truth. However, he warns against offering hospitality to those who bring false teachings, as doing so would be tantamount to participating in their wicked deeds.

The epistle concludes with a hopeful note, expressing John's desire to visit the congregation in person and to have a face-to-face conversation, as there are some matters he prefers not to address through writing. This personal touch underscores the deep concern John had for the spiritual well-being of the believers he addressed.

Overall, the Second Epistle of John serves as a powerful reminder of the importance of adhering to the truth of Christ's teachings, maintaining a life of love and obedience, and being discerning about false teachings that could lead believers astray. Its compact nature makes it a concise yet impactful exhortation to stand firm in the faith.

KEY EVENTS, CHARACTERS, AND TEACHINGS:

- The affirmation of the incarnation of Christ and the warning against false teachers who deny this truth (2 John 1:7)

- The command to love one another and to walk according to God's commandments (2 John 1:5-6)

- The caution against associating with or supporting those who bring false teachings (2 John 1:10-11)

- The encouragement to extend hospitality to fellow believers who are faithful to the truth (2 John 1:10)

- The expression of desire to visit the congregation in person for further discussion (2 John 1:12)

EXPLORING SOME DEEPER MEANINGS:

1. The phrase "the elect lady and her children" is believed to be a metaphorical reference to a specific church congregation and its members. This metaphor emphasizes the close familial relationship among believers and their collective identity as God's chosen people.

2. The repetition of the phrase "walk in the truth" underscores the importance of living a life that is consistent with the teachings of Christ and the apostles. It is not merely intellectual assent but a practical application of the truth in daily living.

3. The concept of "love" is closely linked to obedience to God's commandments. John presents love not merely as an emotion but as a concrete expression of obedience to God's will, particularly in maintaining sound doctrine and rejecting false teachings.

4. The warning against associating with or supporting false teachers is a strong admonition to maintain doctrinal purity and avoid any complicity in spreading deceptive teachings. John emphasizes the importance of discernment and separation from those who distort the truth.

5. The emphasis on hospitality reflects the cultural importance of extending warmth and kindness to fellow believers, particularly those who were traveling and teaching the truth. However, this hospitality was not to be extended to those who promoted false doctrines, as doing so would be seen as endorsing their erroneous beliefs.

6. The personal touch expressed in John's desire to visit the congregation in person highlights the relational aspect of Christian fellowship and the importance of face-to-face communication in addressing sensitive matters.

7. The brevity of the epistle does not diminish its significance, as it encapsulates essential teachings on the importance of adhering to the truth, maintaining love and obedience, and exercising discernment against false teachings.

8. The epistle's emphasis on the truth of Christ's incarnation and the rejection of false teachings that denied this doctrine underscores the centrality of this doctrine to the Christian faith and its importance in combating early heresies.

9. The call to love one another and walk according to God's commandments echoes the teachings of John's other writings, particularly the Gospel of John and the First Epistle of John, reinforcing the consistent message of love, obedience, and adherence to the truth.

10. The epistle's warning against false teachers and the instruction to avoid associating with them highlights the importance of spiritual discernment and the need to protect the purity of the church from deceptive influences that could lead believers astray.

3 John

BOOK SUMMARY:

The Third Epistle of John, a brief yet profound letter, is believed to have been written by the apostle John to his dear friend Gaius. This epistle serves as a commendation of Gaius's faithfulness and hospitality, while also addressing issues of authority, truth, and the importance of supporting those who preach the gospel.

In this concise letter, John expresses his joy and gratitude for Gaius's steadfast commitment to the truth and his willingness to extend hospitality to fellow believers who are traveling and teaching the word of God. John praises Gaius's reputation for walking in the truth and encourages him to continue in this path, emphasizing the importance of supporting those who labor for the sake of the gospel.

John also addresses the matter of authority within the church, confronting the actions of a certain individual named Diotrephes, who had opposed John's authority and refused to welcome traveling preachers. John condemns Diotrephes' behavior as arrogant and divisive, warning Gaius against following such harmful examples.

In contrast, John commends another individual named Demetrius, whose good character and faithfulness to the truth are affirmed. John presents Demetrius as a positive example to emulate, encouraging Gaius to imitate what is good and to continue in his faithful service to the Lord.

The epistle concludes with John's expression of desire to visit Gaius in person and to discuss matters more fully face-to-face. This personal touch underscores the close relationship between John and Gaius, as well as the

importance of personal interaction and fellowship within
the body of Christ.

Overall, the Third Epistle of John serves as a powerful
exhortation to remain faithful to the truth, to support those
who preach the gospel, and to reject divisive and arrogant
behaviors that undermine the unity and witness of the
church.

KEY EVENTS, CHARACTERS, AND TEACHINGS:

- The commendation of Gaius for his faithfulness,
hospitality, and commitment to the truth (3 John 1:1-4)

- The encouragement to support and show hospitality to
traveling preachers and ministers (3 John 1:5-8)

- The condemnation of Diotrephes' arrogant and divisive
behavior, including his rejection of John's authority and
refusal to welcome fellow believers (3 John 1:9-10)

- The affirmation of Demetrius as a positive example of
good character and faithfulness to the truth (3 John 1:12)

- The exhortation to imitate what is good and to avoid
following harmful examples (3 John 1:11)

- The expression of John's desire to visit Gaius in person
for further discussion (3 John 1:13-14)

- The emphasis on the importance of supporting those
who labor for the sake of the gospel and the truth (3 John
1:7-8)

- The warning against divisive and arrogant behaviors that undermine the unity and witness of the church (3 John 1:9-10)

- The affirmation of the importance of maintaining a good reputation and walking in the truth (3 John 1:12)

- The encouragement to extend hospitality and support to fellow believers, particularly those who are traveling and teaching the word of God (3 John 1:5-8)

- The emphasis on the authority of the apostles and the need to respect and submit to their teachings and leadership (3 John 1:9-10)

- The call to imitate good examples and to reject harmful influences that could lead believers astray (3 John 1:11)

EXPLORING SOME DEEPER MEANINGS:

1. The commendation of Gaius's faithfulness and hospitality highlights the importance of supporting and encouraging fellow believers who are laboring for the sake of the gospel. John emphasizes the value of practical acts of service and hospitality as a means of furthering the work of the ministry.

2. The condemnation of Diotrephes' behavior serves as a warning against pride, arrogance, and divisive actions within the church. John's rebuke underscores the need for humility, submission to apostolic authority, and a commitment to maintaining unity among believers.

3. The affirmation of Demetrius as a positive example encourages believers to emulate those who demonstrate good character and faithfulness to the truth. John presents

Demetrius as a role model, emphasizing the importance of living a life that is consistent with the teachings of Christ.

4. The emphasis on supporting and showing hospitality to traveling preachers and ministers reflects the cultural importance of extending warmth and kindness to fellow believers, particularly those who are spreading the gospel message. John highlights the vital role that such hospitality plays in furthering the work of the ministry.

5. The personal touch expressed in John's desire to visit Gaius in person highlights the relational aspect of Christian fellowship and the importance of face-to-face communication in addressing sensitive matters and providing further guidance.

6. The brevity of the epistle does not diminish its significance, as it encapsulates essential teachings on the importance of faithfulness, hospitality, submission to apostolic authority, and the rejection of divisive and arrogant behaviors that undermine the unity of the church.

7. The emphasis on walking in the truth and maintaining a good reputation underscores the importance of living a life that is consistent with the teachings of Christ and the apostles, both in belief and in practical application.

8. The warning against divisive and arrogant behaviors that undermine the unity and witness of the church highlights the importance of humility, submission, and a commitment to preserving the unity of the body of Christ.

9. The affirmation of the importance of supporting those who labor for the sake of the gospel and the truth emphasizes the vital role that practical support and encouragement play in furthering the work of the ministry.

10. The call to imitate good examples and reject harmful influences reflects the need for discernment and the ability to distinguish between positive and negative influences within the church. John encourages believers to follow the example of those who demonstrate faithfulness and good character, while avoiding those who promote divisiveness and harmful behaviors.

Jude:

BOOK SUMMARY:

The Epistle of Jude, written by Jude, the brother of James and a servant of Jesus Christ, is a powerful and impassioned letter that addresses the urgent need to contend for the faith against false teachers and apostasy within the early church.

Jude's primary purpose is to alert believers to the presence of ungodly individuals who have infiltrated the church, propagating false doctrines and promoting moral corruption. These deceivers are described as denying the sovereignty of Christ, indulging in immoral behaviors, and causing divisions within the body of believers.

The epistle begins with a call to earnestly contend for the faith once for all entrusted to the saints, emphasizing the need to defend the purity of the gospel against those who distort its teachings for their own selfish gain.

Jude draws upon vivid examples from the Old Testament to illustrate the severity of God's judgment on those who rebel against His authority. He cites the rebellion of the Israelites in the wilderness, the disobedience of the angels who abandoned their proper domain, and the depravity of the cities of Sodom and Gomorrah as warnings against the consequences of following these false teachers.

Throughout the letter, Jude employs powerful imagery and metaphors to describe the character and actions of these deceivers. He likens them to hidden reefs, clouds without water, and wandering stars, emphasizing their deceptive nature and ultimate futility.

Jude also exhorts believers to build themselves up in the most holy faith, to pray in the Holy Spirit, and to keep themselves in the love of God. He encourages them to have mercy on those who are doubting, while showing discernment and exercising caution in their interactions with those who have embraced false teachings.

The epistle concludes with a doxology, praising God for His ability to keep believers from stumbling and to present them blameless before His glorious presence with great joy.

Overall, the Epistle of Jude serves as a passionate call to contend for the purity of the faith, to reject false teachings and immoral influences, and to remain steadfast in the truth of the gospel, trusting in God's power to preserve and sanctify His people.

KEY EVENTS, CHARACTERS, AND TEACHINGS:

- The call to contend earnestly for the faith once for all entrusted to the saints (Jude 1:3-4)

- The warning against ungodly individuals who have crept into the church, denying Christ and promoting immorality (Jude 1:4)

- The examples of God's judgment on rebellion, disobedience, and immorality, including the Israelites in the wilderness, the fallen angels, and the cities of Sodom and Gomorrah (Jude 1:5-7)

- The vivid descriptions of the false teachers as hidden reefs, clouds without water, and wandering stars (Jude 1:12-13)

- The prophecy of Enoch concerning the Lord's coming to judge the ungodly (Jude 1:14-15)

- The exhortation to build oneself up in the faith, pray in the Holy Spirit, and keep oneself in the love of God (Jude 1:20-21)

- The call to show mercy and discernment in dealing with those who are doubting or embracing false teachings (Jude 1:22-23)

- The doxology praising God for His ability to keep believers from stumbling and to present them blameless before His presence (Jude 1:24-25)

EXPLORING SOME DEEPER MEANINGS:

1. The urgency of Jude's call to "contend earnestly for the faith" underscores the grave threat posed by false teachers and the importance of defending the truth of the gospel against distortion and corruption.

2. The vivid descriptions of the false teachers as "hidden reefs," "clouds without water," and "wandering stars" highlight their deceptive nature and their inability to provide true spiritual nourishment or guidance.

3. The examples of God's judgment on rebellion, disobedience, and immorality serve as powerful warnings against following the path of these false teachers, emphasizing the severe consequences of rejecting God's authority.

4. The prophecy of Enoch, cited by Jude, lends an authoritative voice to the impending judgment on the ungodly, reinforcing the gravity of their actions and the certainty of God's justice.

5. The exhortation to build oneself up in the faith, pray in the Holy Spirit, and keep oneself in the love of God emphasizes the importance of spiritual growth, reliance on the Holy Spirit, and maintaining a close relationship with God as safeguards against deception.

6. The call to show mercy and discernment in dealing with those who are doubting or embracing false teachings highlights the need for a balanced approach, combining compassion with wise judgment and spiritual discernment.

7. The doxology praising God for His ability to keep believers from stumbling and to present them blameless reflects Jude's confidence in God's sovereignty and His power to preserve His people amidst the challenges and threats posed by false teachers.

8. The epistle's urgent tone and passionate language underscore the gravity of the situation facing the early church and the need for immediate action to combat the spread of false teachings and apostasy.

9. Jude's use of vivid imagery and examples from the Old Testament demonstrates his deep knowledge of Scripture and his ability to draw upon its rich tapestry of narratives to reinforce his warnings and exhortations.

10. The emphasis on contending for the faith and maintaining doctrinal purity reflects the high value placed on sound doctrine within the early church and the recognition that false teachings posed a serious threat to the integrity and witness of the Christian community.

Revelation

The Book of Revelation, also known as the Apocalypse, is the final book of the New Testament canon. Authored by the apostle John, this prophetic masterpiece unveils a breathtaking vision of the climactic events of human history and the ultimate triumph of God's Kingdom over evil.

Revelation begins with a prologue that introduces the book as a revelation from Jesus Christ, given to John while exiled on the island of Patmos. It then transitions into a series of letters addressed to seven churches in Asia Minor, exhorting them to remain faithful amidst persecution and to overcome spiritual complacency.

The heart of the book unfolds in a series of visions and symbolic imagery, depicting the cosmic conflict between God and the forces of evil. John witnesses the unfolding of the seven seals, revealing catastrophic events that precede the end times. This is followed by the sounding of seven trumpets, announcing further judgments upon the earth.

Central to the narrative is the appearance of the Lamb, a symbol of Jesus Christ, who alone is worthy to open the seals and initiate the events leading to the establishment of God's eternal Kingdom. John also witnesses the cosmic battle between the forces of good and evil, personified by the dragon (Satan) and the woman (representing God's people).

The book introduces vivid imagery, such as the four horsemen of the Apocalypse, the mark of the beast, and the great harlot, representing the idolatrous systems that oppose God's sovereignty. These symbols have captivated readers throughout the ages and have been the subject of extensive interpretation and debate.

Amidst the turmoil and judgment, John also witnesses the glorious vision of the New Jerusalem, a symbolic representation of the eternal dwelling place of God's redeemed people. This heavenly city is described in breathtaking detail, depicting the ultimate restoration of all things and the fulfillment of God's redemptive plan.

The book concludes with a series of warnings, blessings, and promises, including the assurance of Christ's imminent return and the establishment of His everlasting Kingdom. Revelation stands as a powerful testimony to the sovereignty of God, the certainty of His judgment on sin, and the ultimate victory of the Lamb over the forces of darkness.

KEY EVENTS, CHARACTERS, AND TEACHINGS:

- The letters to the seven churches in Asia Minor, addressing their spiritual condition and exhorting them to repentance and faithfulness (Revelation 2-3)

- The vision of the heavenly throne room and the worship of the Lamb (Revelation 4-5)

- The opening of the seven seals, revealing catastrophic events and judgments (Revelation 6)

- The sealing of the 144,000 from the tribes of Israel and the vision of the multitude in white robes (Revelation 7)

- The sounding of the seven trumpets, announcing further judgments upon the earth (Revelation 8-11)

- The cosmic battle between the woman and the dragon (Satan), and the persecution of God's people (Revelation 12)

- The rise of the beast from the sea and the beast from the earth, representing the antichrist and the false prophet (Revelation 13)

- The vision of the 144,000 redeemed ones standing with the Lamb on Mount Zion (Revelation 14)

- The seven bowls of God's wrath, containing the final judgments upon the earth (Revelation 15-16)

- The fall of Babylon the Great, symbolizing the judgment on the idolatrous and corrupt systems of the world (Revelation 17-18)

- The second coming of Christ, the defeat of the beast and the false prophet, and the binding of Satan (Revelation 19-20)

- The vision of the new heaven and the new earth, and the descent of the New Jerusalem (Revelation 21-22)

- The River of Life, the Tree of Life, and the promise of Christ's imminent return (Revelation 22)

EXPLORING SOME DEEPER MEANINGS:

1. The symbolism of the seven churches in Asia Minor represents the universal church throughout history, with their strengths, weaknesses, and challenges mirroring the spiritual condition of believers in different eras.

2. The vivid imagery of the heavenly throne room and the worship of the Lamb emphasizes the sovereignty and worthiness of God and Christ, setting the stage for the unfolding of God's redemptive plan.

3. The opening of the seven seals signifies the successive stages of God's judgment upon the earth, culminating in the final events leading to the establishment of His Kingdom.

4. The sealing of the 144,000 from the tribes of Israel and the vision of the multitude in white robes represent the preservation and ultimate salvation of God's people, both Jews and Gentiles.

5. The sounding of the seven trumpets introduces a series of escalating judgments upon the earth, symbolizing the increasing intensity of God's wrath upon a rebellious world.

6. The cosmic battle between the woman and the dragon depicts the ongoing conflict between God's people and the forces of evil, led by Satan, throughout history.

7. The rise of the beast from the sea and the beast from the earth symbolize the antichrist and the false prophet, representing the ultimate manifestation of evil and deception in the end times.

8. The vision of the 144,000 redeemed ones standing with the Lamb on Mount Zion represents the victorious and faithful remnant of God's people who have endured persecution and trials.

9. The seven bowls of God's wrath contain the final and most severe judgments upon the earth, signaling the imminent establishment of God's eternal Kingdom.

10. The fall of Babylon the Great symbolizes the judgment upon the idolatrous and corrupt systems of the world that

have opposed God's sovereignty and persecuted His
people.

11. The second coming of Christ, the defeat of the beast
and the false prophet, and the binding of Satan represent
the ultimate triumph of God over evil and the fulfillment of
His redemptive plan.

12. The vision of the new heaven and the new earth, and
the descent of the New Jerusalem, symbolize the eternal
dwelling place of God's redeemed people and the
restoration of all things to their intended perfection.

13. The River of Life and the Tree of Life represent the
eternal sustenance and life-giving provision that will be
available in the new creation, where God's people will
dwell in His presence forever.

14. The promise of Christ's imminent return serves as a
source of hope and encouragement for believers,
reminding them to remain vigilant and faithful in
anticipation of His coming.

Conclusion

Congratulations on completing "A Yearlong Bible Study Guide for Beginners: 52 Week Bible Summary of Scripture". As you reflect on this yearlong journey through the Bible, take a moment to celebrate the progress you've made and the insights you've gained. This guide was designed to help you understand the breadth and depth of Scripture, offering you a clearer picture of God's unfolding story of redemption and love.

Reflecting on the Journey

Over the past year, you've explored the narrative arc of the Bible, from the creation in Genesis to the fulfillment of God's promises in Revelation. You've delved into the lives of pivotal figures like Abraham, Moses, David, and Jesus, and witnessed the faithfulness of God across generations. You've explored profound teachings and doctrines, wrestling with questions of faith, morality, and purpose.

Throughout this journey, you've not only gained knowledge but also grown in your relationship with God. By engaging with the Bible's teachings, reflecting on its messages, and applying its truths to your life, you've taken significant steps in your spiritual growth.

Key Takeaways

- God's Faithfulness: From the promises to Abraham to the birth of the early church, God's faithfulness is evident throughout Scripture. His promises are steadfast, and His love endures forever.

- The Role of Jesus: The life, death, and resurrection of Jesus Christ are central to the biblical narrative. Understanding His role as Savior and Redeemer is crucial to comprehending the Bible's message of salvation.

- The Power of Faith: The stories of biblical figures demonstrate the power and importance of faith. Whether through trials or triumphs, faith in God's promises leads to transformation and fulfillment.

- The Call to Love and Serve: The Bible consistently calls believers to love God and others, serving as a reflection of Christ's love in the world. This call is central to the life of a Christian and the mission of the church.

Continuing the Journey

Completing this guide is not the end but a milestone in your spiritual journey. As you continue to explore and study the Bible, consider the following ways to deepen your engagement with Scripture:

- Join a Study Group: Sharing insights and discussions with others can enrich your understanding and offer new perspectives.

- Seek Further Resources: Explore our page and socials for more commentaries, theological books, and online courses to expand your knowledge of biblical texts and themes.

- Apply What You've Learned: Let the teachings of the Bible shape your actions, relationships, and decisions. Live out the principles and values you've discovered in your study.

- Continue in Prayer: Maintain a strong prayer life, seeking God's guidance and wisdom as you apply His Word to your life.

Final Thoughts

The Bible is an inexhaustible source of wisdom, encouragement, and inspiration. As you continue your journey, may you find renewed strength and purpose in its pages. Remember that Scripture is not just a collection of ancient writings but a living and active guide for life today.

Thank you for choosing this guide as your companion through the Bible. May it continue to be a resource you return to for insight and encouragement in the years to come.

May God bless you richly as you continue to seek His truth and live out His Word.

In faith and fellowship,

Rev Minton Thomas

Glossary

Abomination: An action or object that is detestable and offensive to God, often referring to idolatry or immoral practices.

Apostle: A messenger and ambassador, specifically chosen by Jesus Christ to spread the Gospel. Paul, for example, is an apostle called to preach to the Gentiles.

Ark of the Covenant: A sacred chest containing the tablets of the Ten Commandments, representing God's presence and covenant with Israel.

Atonement: The reconciliation of God and humankind through the sacrificial death of Jesus Christ.

Baptism: A Christian sacrament signifying spiritual cleansing and rebirth, involving immersion in or sprinkling with water as an outward sign of inward faith.

Covenant: A solemn agreement or contract between God and humans. In the Old Testament, covenants include those with Noah, Abraham, and Moses; in the New Testament, the New Covenant is through Jesus Christ.

Decalogue: Another term for the Ten Commandments, the core ethical guidelines given by God to Moses on Mount Sinai.

Flesh: Human nature in its fallen state, prone to sin and opposed to the Spirit. It contrasts with the spiritual life led by the Holy Spirit.

Foreshadowing: A literary technique that hints at future events in a narrative, especially the coming of the messiah.

Fruit of the Spirit: Characteristics and virtues produced in the life of a believer by the Holy Spirit, such as love, joy, peace, patience, kindness, goodness, faithfulness, gentleness, and self-control.

Genealogy: A record or account of the ancestry and descent of a person, family, or group.

Gentile: A person who is not of Jewish descent. In the New Testament, Gentiles are included in the Gospel message alongside Jews.

Gospel: The "good news" of Jesus Christ, including His death, resurrection, and the salvation offered through faith in Him.

Idolatry: The worship of idols or other gods, considered a grave sin and violation of the first commandment in the Old Testament.

Insurmountable: Unable to be overcome or surmounted; insuperable.

Israel: The name given to Jacob and, by extension, his descendants, forming the nation chosen by God to fulfill His purposes.

Judges: Leaders raised up by God to deliver Israel from oppression and govern the people before the establishment of the monarchy.

Levites: Members of the tribe of Levi, set apart for religious duties and the service of the tabernacle and, later, the temple.

Manna: The miraculous food provided by God to the Israelites during their journey through the wilderness.

Messiah: An anointed one or savior promised in the Old Testament, anticipated as the deliverer of Israel.

Messianic: Relating to the Messiah or a savior figure in religious belief.

Mosaic Covenant: The agreement between God and the Israelites as mediated through Moses, typically associated with the giving of the Law.

Oracles: Divine communications or revelations, often delivered through a medium or prophet.

Parallelism: A literary device in Hebrew poetry where ideas are expressed in two or more lines that correspond in structure, content, or both.

Passover: A Jewish festival commemorating the Exodus from Egypt, marked by the sacrifice of a lamb and the eating of unleavened bread.

Pentateuch: The first five books of the Bible (Genesis, Exodus, Leviticus, Numbers, Deuteronomy), traditionally attributed to Moses.

Pharaoh: The title of the king of Egypt, often depicted as an adversary in the Exodus narrative.

Prophecy: Divinely inspired utterance or revelation, typically predicting future events.

Prophet: A person chosen by God to deliver His messages and guidance to the people, often calling them to repentance and faithfulness.

Protevangelium: The first announcement of the gospel, typically referring to Genesis 3:15, which is seen as the first prophecy of a savior.

Redemption: The act of being saved from sin, error, or evil, often through divine intervention.

Righteousness: The quality of being morally right or justifiable. In Christianity, it is attributed to believers through faith in Christ, who imparts His righteousness to them.

Sacrifice: An offering made to God, often involving the killing of an animal, as a means of atonement, thanksgiving, or dedication.

Sanctification: The process of being made holy, set apart for God's purposes. It involves spiritual growth and transformation into the likeness of Christ through the work of the Holy Spirit.

Sin: Any action or thought that goes against God's will and law, resulting in separation from God and requiring atonement.

Tabernacle: A portable sanctuary used by the Israelites during their journey in the wilderness, where God's presence dwelt and sacrifices were offered.

Temple: The permanent place of worship built in Jerusalem, serving as the center of Israel's religious life and sacrificial system.

Visions: Supernatural experiences of seeing or perceiving something not physically present, often conveying spiritual truths.